SCHOLASTI

Number and Operations in Base Ten

Understanding • Strategies • Connections

Participant Guide

 Published by Scholastic Inc. Printed in the U.S.A.

ISBN-13: 978-0-545-67425-6
ISBN-10: 0-545-67425-5

3 4 5 6 7 8 9 10 31 23 22 21 20 19 18 17 16 15

Table of Contents

Course Overview 6
Standards for Mathematical Practice 12
Standards for Mathematical Content 16
Supporting Mathematical Thinking 27
Leading Meaningful Discussions 28
Alternative Algorithms 30
Analyzing Students' Thinking: Addition 31
Analyzing Students' Thinking: Subtraction 32
Analyzing Students' Thinking: Multiplication 33
Analyzing Students' Thinking: Division 34
Understanding Part-Whole Relationships 35
What Do You See? 36
Collect Ten 39
Sums of More Than Ten 44
Spill and Compare 50
Hundred Chart 54
Hundred Chart Puzzle 56
Hippety Hop 58
Look, Quick! 62
Race to 100 64
How Far Away? 71
Guess My Number 73
Scaffolding the Open Number Line 75
101 and Out 77
Types of Addition and Subtraction Word Problems 80
Addition and Subtraction Situations 84
Classifying Addition and Subtraction Word Problems 86
Addition and Subtraction Strategies 88
Learning From Student Work 93
Place-Value Assessment 98
Implementing Effective Routines 99
Breaking Numbers Apart 102
Estimating 104
Grow and Shrink 107

Double Ten-Frame 109
Measuring Area 110
Balancing Number Puzzles 111
Investigating Rectangles 115
Building the Multiplication Chart 118
Silent Multiplication 122
Factor Fiddling 124
Multiplication and Division 125
Analyzing Multiplication and Division Word Problems 126
Two Types of Word Problems 128
Multiplication and Division Situations 134
Classifying Word Problems 136
Division Computation 138
The Divisor Stays the Same 139
The Dividend Stays the Same 140
The Factor Game 141
How Long? How Many? 144
The Game of Leftovers 146
Leftovers With 100 147
Multiplication Bingo 148
Hit the Target 149
Game Reflection Sheets 150
Developing Arithmetic Understanding 153
Procedural Fluency: Alternative Algorithms 159
Promoting Decimal Sense 162
Identifying Aspects of Learning 163
Connecting Multiple Representations 164
Learning From Student Work 167
Mind Map 170
Professional Article: Linking Assessment and Instruction 172
Professional Article: How Children Learn Mathematics 177
Collect Ten Recording Sheet 180
Sums of More Than Ten Recording Sheet 181
Spill and Compare Recording Sheet 183
Scaffolding the Open Number Line 184
101 and Out Recording Sheet 186

The Factor Game Recording Sheet 187
How Long? How Many? Recording Sheet 188
$\frac{1}{2}$-Inch Grid Paper 189
Small 10-by-10 Grids 190
Decimal Representations Recording Sheet 191
$\frac{1}{2}$-Inch Grid Paper 193
Symbols 199
True, False, and Open Sentences 201
Open Sentences 205
True or False Number Sentences 207
Hundred Chart Puzzle Pieces 209
Race to 100 Tens Strips 211
Race to 100 Fives Strips 213
Race to 100 Action Cards 215
Race to 100 Question Cards 217
Sums of More Than Ten Cards 219
Ten-Frame Cards 221

Course Overview

GRADES K–2

Day 1 Agenda

30 minutes	**Opening**
75 minutes	**Examining Addition and Subtraction Strategies**
	Break
75 minutes	**The Power of Ten**
	Lunch
45 minutes	**How Students Learn**
	Break
60 minutes	**Using Appropriate Tools Strategically: Hundred Chart**
15 minutes	**Closing**

Day 2 Agenda

30 minutes	**Opening**
60 minutes	**Using Appropriate Tools Strategically: Number Line**
	Break
75 minutes	**True, False, and Open Sentences**
	Lunch
60 minutes	**Analyzing Types of Word Problems: Addition and Subtraction**
	Break
75 minutes	**Addition and Subtraction Strategies**

Day 3 Agenda

15 minutes	**Opening**
105 minutes	**Linking Assessment and Instruction**
	Break
60 minutes	**Introducing Routines**
	Lunch
90 minutes	**Implementing Routines**
	Break
30 minutes	**Closing**

Learning Outcomes

After the course, participants will be able to:

- Articulate key aspects of the Common Core State Standards of Number and Operations in Base Ten and Operations and Algebraic Thinking for Grades K–2
- Consider instructional shifts needed to foster the depth of understanding communicated in the Common Core State Standards
- Describe the interconnectedness of place value and the base-ten number system to operations and algebraic thinking
- Characterize teaching strategies that exemplify the Common Core State Standards for Mathematical Practices
- Implement instructional strategies including the use of classroom discussions, small-group work, and the use of concrete materials and contexts to support students' learning

GRADES 3–5

Day 1 Agenda

30 minutes	**Opening**
45 minutes	**Extending Place Value: Balancing Number Puzzles**
	Break
90 minutes	**A Geometric Model for Multiplication**
	Lunch
60 minutes	**Exploring Patterns in Factors and Products**
	Break
75 minutes	**Analyzing Types of Word Problems: Multiplication and Division**

Day 2 Agenda

15 minutes	**Opening**
75 minutes	**Division Computation**
	Break
60 minutes	**Patterns With Division**
	Lunch
60 minutes	**Utilizing Games: The Role of the Teacher**
	Break
75 minutes	**Multiplication and Division Menu**
15 minutes	**Closing**

Day 3 Agenda

10 minutes	**Opening**
70 minutes	**True, False, and Open Sentences**
	Break
90 minutes	**Procedural Fluency: Alternative Algorithms**
	Lunch
45 minutes	**Promoting Decimal Number Sense**
	Break
60 minutes	**Linking Assessment and Instruction**
30 minutes	**Closing**

Learning Outcomes

After the course, participants will be able to:

- Articulate key aspects of the Common Core State Standards of Number and Operations in Base Ten and Operations and Algebraic Thinking for Grades 3–5
- Consider instructional shifts needed to foster the depth of understanding communicated in the Common Core State Standards
- Describe the interconnectedness of place value and the base-ten number system to operations and algebraic thinking
- Characterize teaching strategies that exemplify the Common Core State Standards for Mathematical Practices
- Implement instructional strategies including the use of classroom discussions, small-group work, and the use of concrete materials and contexts to support students' learning

GRADES K–5

Day 1 Agenda

30 minutes	**Opening**
75 minutes	**The Power of Ten**
	Break
45 minutes	**Extending Place Value: Balancing Number Puzzles**
	Lunch
90 minutes	**A Geometric Model for Multiplication**
	Break
55 minutes	**Exploring Patterns in Factors and Products**
10 minutes	**Closing**

Day 2 Agenda

15 minutes	**Opening**
60 minutes	**Using Appropriate Tools Strategically: Hundred Chart**
	Break
60 minutes	**Division Computation**
	Lunch
60 minutes	**Using Appropriate Tools Strategically: Number Line**
	Break
75 minutes	**True, False, and Open Sentences**
15 minutes	**Closing**

Day 3 Agenda

15 minutes	**Opening**
75 minutes	**Analyzing Word Problems**
	Break
90 minutes	**Procedural Fluency: Alternative Algorithms**
	Lunch
75 minutes	**Linking Assessment and Instruction**
	Break
30 minutes	**Closing**

Standards for Mathematical Practice

The Common Core State Standards for Mathematical Practice represent mathematical habits of mind that all students require for college and career readiness.

Background on the Practices

The Common Core State Standards for Mathematical Practice describe varieties of expertise that mathematics educators at all levels should seek to develop in their students. These practices rest on processes and proficiencies with long-standing importance in mathematics education. The first of these processes and proficiencies are the National Council of Teachers of Mathematics (NCTM) process standards of problem solving, reasoning and proof, communication, representation, and connections. The second are the strands of mathematical proficiency specified in the National Research Council's report *Adding It Up*: adaptive reasoning, strategic competence, conceptual understanding (comprehension of mathematical concepts, operations, and relations), procedural fluency (skill in carrying out procedures flexibly, accurately, efficiently, and appropriately), and productive disposition (habitual inclination to see mathematics as sensible, useful, and worthwhile, coupled with a belief in diligence and one's own efficacy).

1. Make sense of problems and persevere in solving them.

Mathematically proficient students start by explaining to themselves the meaning of a problem and looking for entry points to its solution. They analyze givens, constraints, relationships, and goals. They make conjectures about the form and meaning of the solution and plan a solution pathway rather than simply jumping into a solution attempt. They consider analogous problems, and try special cases and simpler forms of the original problem in order to gain insight into its solution. They monitor and evaluate their progress and change course if necessary.

Older students might, depending on the context of the problem, transform algebraic expressions or change the viewing window on their graphing calculators to get the information they need. Mathematically proficient students can explain correspondences between equations, verbal descriptions, tables, and graphs or draw diagrams of important features and relationships, graph data, and search for regularity or trends. Younger students might rely on using concrete objects or pictures to help conceptualize and solve a problem.

Mathematically proficient students check their answers to problems using a different method, and they continually ask themselves, "Does this make sense?" They can understand the approaches of others to solving complex problems and identify correspondences between different approaches.

2. Reason abstractly and quantitatively.

Mathematically proficient students make sense of quantities and their relationships in problem situations. They bring two complementary abilities to bear on problems involving quantitative relationships: the ability to *decontextualize*—to abstract a given situation and represent it symbolically and manipulate the representing symbols as if they have a life of their own, without necessarily attending to their referents—and the ability to *contextualize*—to pause as needed during the manipulation process in order to probe into the referents for the symbols involved.

Quantitative reasoning entails habits of creating a coherent representation of the problem at hand; considering the units involved; attending to the meaning of quantities, not just how to compute them; and knowing and flexibly using different properties of operations and objects.

3. Construct viable arguments and critique the reasoning of others.

Mathematically proficient students understand and use stated assumptions, definitions, and previously established results in constructing arguments. They make conjectures and build a logical progression of statements to explore the truth of their conjectures. They are able to analyze situations by breaking them into cases, and can recognize and use counterexamples. They justify their conclusions, communicate them to others, and respond to the arguments of others. They reason inductively about data, making plausible arguments that take into account the context from which the data arose.

Mathematically proficient students are also able to compare the effectiveness of two plausible arguments, distinguish correct logic or reasoning from that which is flawed, and—if there is a flaw in an argument—explain what it is. Elementary students can construct arguments using concrete referents such as objects, drawings, diagrams, and actions. Such arguments can make sense and be correct, even though they are not generalized or made formal until later grades. Later, students learn to determine domains to which an argument applies. Students at all grades can listen to or read the arguments of others, decide whether they make sense, and ask useful questions to clarify or improve the arguments.

4. Model with mathematics.

Mathematically proficient students can apply the mathematics they know to solve problems arising in everyday life, society, and the workplace. In early grades, this might be as simple as writing an addition equation to describe a situation. In middle grades, a student might apply proportional reasoning to plan a school event or analyze a problem in the community. By high school, a student might use geometry to solve a design problem or use a function to describe how one quantity of interest depends on another.

Mathematically proficient students who can apply what they know are comfortable making assumptions and approximations to simplify a complicated situation, realizing that these may need revision later. They are able to identify important quantities in a practical situation and map their relationships using such tools as diagrams, two-way tables, graphs, flow charts, and formulas. They can analyze those relationships mathematically to draw conclusions. They routinely interpret their mathematical results in the context of the situation and reflect on whether the results make sense, possibly improving the model if it has not served its purpose.

5. Use appropriate tools strategically.

Mathematically proficient students consider the available tools when solving a mathematical problem. These tools might include pencil and paper, concrete models, a ruler, a protractor, a calculator, a spreadsheet, a computer algebra system, a statistical package, or dynamic geometry software.

Proficient students are sufficiently familiar with tools appropriate for their grades or courses to make sound decisions about when each of these tools might be helpful, recognizing both the insight to be gained and the tools' limitations. For example, mathematically proficient high school students analyze graphs of functions and solutions generated using a graphing calculator. They detect possible errors by strategically using estimation and other mathematical knowledge. When making mathematical models, they know that technology can enable them to visualize the results of varying assumptions, explore consequences, and compare predictions with data.

Mathematically proficient students at various grade levels are able to identify relevant external mathematical resources, such as digital content located on a website, and use them to pose or solve problems. They are able to use technological tools to explore and deepen their understanding of concepts.

6. **Attend to precision.**

Mathematically proficient students try to communicate precisely to others. They try to use clear definitions in discussion with others and in their own reasoning. They state the meaning of the symbols they choose, including using the equal sign consistently and appropriately. They are careful about specifying units of measure and labeling axes to clarify the correspondence with quantities in a problem. They calculate accurately and efficiently, and express numerical answers with a degree of precision appropriate for the problem context. In the elementary grades, students give carefully formulated explanations to each other. By the time they reach high school, they have learned to examine claims and make explicit use of definitions.

7. **Look for and make use of structure.**

Mathematically proficient students look closely to discern a pattern or structure. Young students, for example, might notice that three and seven more is the same amount as seven and three more, or they may sort a collection of shapes according to how many sides the shapes have. Later, students will see 7×8 equals the well-remembered $7 \times 5 + 7 \times 3$, in preparation for learning about the distributive property. In the expression $x^2 + 9x + 14$, older students can see the 14 as 2×7 and the 9 as $2 + 7$. They recognize the significance of an existing line in a geometric figure and can use the strategy of drawing an auxiliary line for solving problems. They also can step back for an overview and shift perspective. They can see complicated things, such as some algebraic expressions, as single objects or as being composed of several objects. For example, they can see $5 - 3(x - y)^2$ as 5 minus a positive number times a square and use that to realize that its value cannot be more than 5 for any real numbers x and y.

8. **Look for and express regularity in repeated reasoning.**

Mathematically proficient students notice if calculations are repeated, and look both for general methods and for shortcuts. Upper elementary students might notice when dividing 25 by 11 that they are repeating the same calculations over and over again, and conclude they have a repeating decimal. By paying attention to the calculation of slope as they repeatedly check whether points are on the line passing through (1, 2) with slope 3, middle school students might abstract the equation $(y - 2)/(x - 1) = 3$. Noticing the regularity in the way terms cancel when expanding $(x - 1)(x + 1)$, $(x - 1)(x^2 + x + 1)$, and $(x - 1)(x^3 + x^2 + x + 1)$ might lead them to the general formula for the sum of a geometric series. As they work to solve a problem, mathematically proficient students maintain oversight of the process, while attending to the details. They continually evaluate the reasonableness of their intermediate results.

Standards for Mathematical Content

The Standards for Mathematical Content are divided into domains in Grades K–8. This course focuses on two of the domains: Operations and Algebraic Thinking and Number and Operations in Base Ten.

KINDERGARTEN

Counting and Cardinality

Know number names and the count sequence

K.CC.1 Count to 100 by ones and tens.

K.CC.2 Count forward beginning from a given number within the known sequence (instead of having to begin at 1).

K.CC.3 Write numbers from 0 to 20. Represent a number of objects with a written numeral 0–20 (with 0 representing a count of no objects).

Count to tell the number of objects

K.CC.4 Understand the relationship between numbers and quantities; connect counting to cardinality.

- **K.CC.4a** When counting objects, say the number names in the standard order, pairing each object with one and only one number name and each number name with one and only one object.
- **K.CC.4b** Understand that the last number name said tells the number of objects counted. The number of objects is the same regardless of their arrangement or the order in which they were counted.
- **K.CC.4c** Understand that each successive number name refers to a quantity that is one larger.

K.CC.5 Count to answer "how many?" questions about as many as 20 things arranged in a line, a rectangular array, or a circle, or as many as 10 things in a scattered configuration; given a number from 1–20, count out that many objects.

Compare numbers

K.CC.6 Identify whether the number of objects in one group is greater than, less than, or equal to the number of objects in another group (e.g., by using matching and counting strategies).

K.CC.7 Compare two numbers between 1 and 10 presented as written numerals.

Operations and Algebraic Thinking

Understand addition as putting together and adding to, and understand subtraction as taking apart and taking from.

K.OA.1 Represent addition and subtraction with objects, fingers, mental objects, drawings, sounds (e.g., claps), acting out situations, verbal explanations, expressions, or equations.

K.OA.2 Solve addition and subtraction word problems, and add and subtract within 10 (e.g., by using objects or drawings to represent the problem).

K.OA.3 Decompose numbers less than or equal to 10 into pairs in more than one way (e.g., by using objects or drawings), and record each decomposition by a drawing or equation (e.g., $5 = 2 + 3$ and $5 = 4 + 1$).

K.OA.4 For any given number from 1 to 9, find the number that makes 10 when added to the given number (e.g., by using objects or drawings), and record the answer with a drawing or equation.

K.OA.5 Fluently add and subtract within 5.

Number and Operations in Base Ten

K.NBT.1 Compose and decompose numbers from 11 to 19 into ten ones and some further ones (e.g., by using objects or drawings), and record each composition or decomposition by a drawing or equation (e.g., $18 = 10 + 8$); understand that these numbers are composed of ten ones and one, two, three, four, five, six, seven, eight, or nine ones.

GRADE 1

Operations and Algebraic Thinking

Represent and solve problems involving addition and subtraction.

1.OA.1 Use addition and subtraction within 20 to solve word problems involving situations of adding to, taking from, putting together, taking apart, and comparing, with unknowns in all positions (e.g., by using objects, drawings, and equations with a symbol for the unknown number to represent the problem).

1.OA.2 Solve word problems that call for addition of three whole numbers whose sum is less than or equal to 20 (e.g., by using objects, drawings, and equations with a symbol for the unknown number to represent the problem).

Understand and apply properties of operations and the relationship between addition and subtraction.

1.OA.3 Apply properties of operations as strategies to add and subtract. *Examples: If $8 + 3 = 11$ is known, then $3 + 8 = 11$ is also known. (Commutative property of addition.) To add $2 + 6 + 4$, the second two numbers can be added to make a ten, so $2 + 6 + 4 = 2 + 10 = 12$. (Associative property of addition.)*

1.OA.4 Understand subtraction as an unknown-addend problem. *For example, subtract $10 - 8$ by finding the number that makes 10 when added to 8.*

Add and subtract within 20.

1.OA.5 Relate counting to addition and subtraction (e.g., by counting 2 to add 2).

1.OA.6 Add and subtract within 20, demonstrating fluency for addition and subtraction within 10. Use strategies such as counting on; making ten (e.g., $8 + 6 = 8 + 2 + 4 = 10 + 4 = 14$); decomposing a number leading to a ten (e.g., $13 - 4 = 13 - 3 - 1 = 10 - 1 = 9$); using the relationship between addition and subtraction (e.g., knowing that $8 + 4 = 12$, one knows $12 - 8 = 4$); and creating equivalent but easier or known sums (e.g., adding $6 + 7$ by creating the known equivalent $6 + 6 + 1 = 12 + 1 = 13$).

Work with addition and subtraction equations.

1.OA.7 Understand the meaning of the equal sign, and determine if equations involving addition and subtraction are true or false. *For example, which of the following equations are true and which are false? $6 = 6$, $7 = 8 - 1$, $5 + 2 = 2 + 5$, $4 + 1 = 5 + 2$.*

1.OA.8 Determine the unknown whole number in an addition or subtraction equation relating three whole numbers. *For example, determine the unknown number that makes the equation true in each of the equations $8 + ? = 11$, $5 = \_ - 3$, $6 + 6 = \_$.*

Number and Operations in Base Ten

Extend the counting sequence.

1.NBT.1 Count to 120, starting at any number less than 120. In this range, read and write numerals and represent a number of objects with a written numeral.

Understand place value.

1.NBT.2 Understand that the two digits of a two-digit number represent amounts of tens and ones. Understand the following as special cases:

1.NBT.2a 10 can be thought of as a bundle of ten ones, called a "ten."

1.NBT.2b The numbers from 11 to 19 are composed of a ten and one, two, three, four, five, six, seven, eight, or nine ones.

1.NBT.2c The numbers 10, 20, 30, 40, 50, 60, 70, 80, 90 refer to one, two, three, four, five, six, seven, eight, or nine tens (and 0 ones).

1.NBT.3 Compare two two-digit numbers based on meanings of the tens and ones digits, recording the results of comparisons with the symbols $>$, $=$, and $<$.

Use place-value understanding and properties of operations to add and subtract.

1.NBT.4 Add within 100, including adding a two-digit number and a one-digit number, and adding a two-digit number and a multiple of 10, using concrete models or drawings and strategies based on place value, properties of operations, and/or the relationship between addition and subtraction; relate the strategy to a written method and explain the reasoning used. Understand that in adding two-digit numbers, one adds tens and tens, ones and ones; and sometimes it is necessary to compose a ten.

1.NBT.5 Given a two-digit number, mentally find 10 more or 10 less than the number, without having to count; explain the reasoning used.

1.NBT.6 Subtract multiples of 10 in the range 10–90 from multiples of 10 in the range 10–90 (positive or zero differences), using concrete models or drawings and strategies based on place value, properties of operations, and/or the relationship between addition and subtraction; relate the strategy to a written method and explain the reasoning used.

GRADE 2

Operations and Algebraic Thinking

Represent and solve problems involving addition and subtraction.

2.OA.1 Use addition and subtraction within 100 to solve one- and two-step word problems involving situations of adding to, taking from, putting together, taking apart, and comparing, with unknowns in all positions (e.g., by using drawings and equations with a symbol for the unknown number to represent the problem).

Add and subtract within 20.

2.OA.2 Fluently add and subtract within 20 using mental strategies. By the end of Grade 2, know from memory all sums of two one-digit numbers.

Work with equal groups of objects to gain foundations for multiplication.

2.OA.3 Determine whether a group of objects (up to 20) has an odd or even number of members (e.g., by pairing objects or counting them by 2s); write an equation to express an even number as a sum of two equal addends.

2.OA.4 Use addition to find the total number of objects arranged in rectangular arrays with up to 5 rows and up to 5 columns; write an equation to express the total as a sum of equal addends.

Number and Operations in Base Ten

Understand place value.

2.NBT.1 Understand that the three digits of a three-digit number represent amounts of hundreds, tens, and ones (e.g., 706 equals 7 hundreds, 0 tens, and 6 ones). Understand the following as special cases:

2.NBT.1a 100 can be thought of as a bundle of ten tens, called a "hundred."

2.NBT.1b The numbers 100, 200, 300, 400, 500, 600, 700, 800, 900 refer to one, two, three, four, five, six, seven, eight, or nine hundreds (and 0 tens and 0 ones).

2.NBT.2 Count within 1000; skip-count by 5s, 10s, and 100s.

2.NBT.3 Read and write numbers to 1000 using base-ten numerals, number names, and expanded form.

2.NBT.4 Compare two three-digit numbers based on meanings of the hundreds, tens, and ones digits, using $>$, $=$, and $<$ symbols to record the results of comparisons.

Use place-value understanding and properties of operations to add and subtract.

2.NBT.5 Fluently add and subtract within 100 using strategies based on place value, properties of operations, and/or the relationship between addition and subtraction.

2.NBT.6 Add up to four two-digit numbers using strategies based on place value and properties of operations.

2.NBT.7 Add and subtract within 1000, using concrete models or drawings and strategies based on place value, properties of operations, and/or the relationship between addition and subtraction; relate the strategy to a written method. Understand that in adding or subtracting three-digit numbers, one adds or subtracts hundreds and hundreds, tens and tens, ones and ones; and sometimes it is necessary to compose or decompose tens or hundreds.

2.NBT.8 Mentally add 10 or 100 to a given number 100–900, and mentally subtract 10 or 100 from a given number 100–900.

2.NBT.9 Explain why addition and subtraction strategies work, using place value and the properties of operations.

GRADE 3

Operations and Algebraic Thinking

Represent and solve problems involving multiplication and division.

3.OA.1 Interpret products of whole numbers (e.g., interpret 5×7 as the total number of objects in 5 groups of 7 objects each). *For example, describe a context in which a total number of objects can be expressed as 5×7.*

3.OA.2 Interpret whole-number quotients of whole numbers (e.g., interpret $56 \div 8$ as the number of objects in each share when 56 objects are partitioned equally into 8 shares, or as a number of shares when 56 objects are partitioned into equal shares of 8 objects each). For example, describe a context in which a number of shares or a number of groups can be expressed as $56 \div 8$.

3.OA.3 Use multiplication and division within 100 to solve word problems in situations involving equal groups, arrays, and measurement quantities (e.g., by using drawings and equations with a symbol for the unknown number to represent the problem).

3.OA.4 Determine the unknown whole number in a multiplication or division equation relating three whole numbers. *For example, determine the unknown number that makes the equation true in each of the equations $8 \times ? = 48$, $5 = \_ \div 3$, $6 \times 6 = ?$.*

Understand properties of multiplication and the relationship between multiplication and division.

3.OA.5 Apply properties of operations as strategies to multiply and divide. *Examples: If $6 \times 4 = 24$ is known, then $4 \times 6 = 24$ is also known. (Commutative property of multiplication.) $3 \times 5 \times 2$ can be found by $3 \times 5 = 15$, then $15 \times 2 = 30$, or by $5 \times 2 = 10$, then $3 \times 10 = 30$. (Associative property of multiplication.) Knowing that $8 \times 5 = 40$ and $8 \times 2 = 16$, one can find 8×7 as $8 \times (5 + 2) = (8 \times 5) + (8 \times 2) = 40 + 16 = 56$. (Distributive property.)*

3.OA.6 Understand division as an unknown-factor problem. *For example, find $32 \div 8$ by finding the number that makes 32 when multiplied by 8.*

Multiply and divide within 100.

3.OA.7 Fluently multiply and divide within 100, using strategies such as the relationship between multiplication and division (e.g., knowing that $8 \times 5 = 40$, one knows $40 \div 5 = 8$) or properties of operations. By the end of Grade 3, know from memory all products of two one-digit numbers.

Solve problems involving the four operations, and identify and explain patterns in arithmetic.

3.OA.8 Solve two-step word problems using the four operations. Represent these problems using equations with a letter standing for the unknown quantity. Assess the reasonableness of answers using mental computation and estimation strategies including rounding.

3.OA.9 Identify arithmetic patterns (including patterns in the addition table or multiplication table), and explain them using properties of operations. *For example, observe that 4 times a number is always even, and explain why 4 times a number can be decomposed into two equal addends.*

Number and Operations in Base Ten

Use place-value understanding and properties of operations to perform multi-digit arithmetic.

3.NBT.1 Use place-value understanding to round whole numbers to the nearest 10 or 100.

3.NBT.2 Fluently add and subtract within 1000 using strategies and algorithms based on place value, properties of operations, and/or the relationship between addition and subtraction.

3.NBT.3 Multiply one-digit whole numbers by multiples of 10 in the range 10–90 (e.g., 9×80, $5 = 60$) using strategies based on place value and properties of operations.

GRADE 4

Operations and Algebraic Thinking

Use the four operations with whole numbers to solve problems.

4.OA.1 Interpret a multiplication equation as a comparison (e.g., interpret $35 = 5 \times 7$ as a statement that 35 is 5 times as many as 7 and 7 times as many as 5). Represent verbal statements of multiplicative comparisons as multiplication equations.

4.OA.2 Multiply or divide to solve word problems involving multiplicative comparison (e.g., by using drawings and equations with a symbol for the unknown number to represent the problem), distinguishing multiplicative comparison from additive comparison.

4.OA.3 Solve multistep word problems posed with whole numbers and having whole-number answers using the four operations, including problems in which remainders must be interpreted. Represent these problems using equations with a letter standing for the unknown quantity. Assess the reasonableness of answers using mental computation and estimation strategies including rounding.

Gain familiarity with factors and multiples.

4.OA.4 Find all factor pairs for a whole number in the range 1–100. Recognize that a whole number is a multiple of each of its factors. Determine whether a given whole number in the range 1–100 is a multiple of a given one-digit number. Determine whether a given whole number in the range 1–100 is prime or composite.

Generate and analyze patterns.

4.OA.5 Generate a number or shape pattern that follows a given rule. Identify apparent features of the pattern that were not explicit in the rule itself. For example, given the rule "Add 3" and the starting number 1, generate terms in the resulting sequence and observe that the terms appear to alternate between odd and even numbers. Explain informally why the numbers will continue to alternate in this way.

Number and Operations in Base Ten

Generalize place-value understanding for multi-digit whole numbers.

4.NBT.1 Recognize that in a multi-digit whole number, a digit in one place represents ten times what it represents in the place to its right. *For example, recognize that $700 \div 70 = 10$ by applying concepts of place value and division.*

4.NBT.2 Read and write multi-digit whole numbers using base-ten numerals, number names, and expanded form. Compare two multi-digit numbers based on meanings of the digits in each place, using $>$, $=$, and $<$ symbols to record the results of comparisons.

4.NBT.3 Use place-value understanding to round multi-digit whole numbers to any place.

Use place-value understanding and properties of operations to perform multi-digit arithmetic.

4.NBT.4 Fluently add and subtract multi-digit whole numbers using the standard algorithms.

4.NBT.5 Multiply a whole number of up to four digits by a one-digit whole number, and multiply two two-digit numbers, using strategies based on place value and the properties of operations. Illustrate and explain the calculation by using equations, rectangular arrays, and/or area models.

4.NBT.6 Find whole-number quotients and remainders with up to four-digit dividends and one-digit divisors, using strategies based on place value, the properties of operations, and/or the relationship between multiplication and division. Illustrate and explain the calculation by using equations, rectangular arrays, and/or area models.

GRADE 5

Operations and Algebraic Thinking

Write and interpret numerical expressions.

5.OA.1 Use parentheses, brackets, or braces in numerical expressions, and evaluate expressions with these symbols.

5.OA.2 Write simple expressions that record calculations with numbers, and interpret numerical expressions without evaluating them. *For example, express the calculation "add 8 and 7, then multiply by 2" as $2 \times (8 + 7)$. Recognize that $3 \times (18932 + 921)$ is three times as large as $18932 + 921$, without having to calculate the indicated sum or product.*

Analyze patterns and relationships.

5.OA.3 Generate two numerical patterns using two given rules. Identify apparent relationships between corresponding terms. Form ordered pairs consisting of corresponding terms from the two patterns, and graph the ordered pairs on a coordinate plane. *For example, given the rule "Add 3" and the starting number 0, and given the rule "Add 6" and the starting number 0, generate terms in the resulting sequences, and observe that the terms in one sequence are twice the corresponding terms in the other sequence. Explain informally why this is so.*

Number and Operations in Base Ten

Understand the place-value system.

5.NBT.1 Recognize that in a multi-digit number, a digit in one place represents 10 times as much as it represents in the place to its right and 1/10 of what it represents in the place to its left.

5.NBT.2 Explain patterns in the number of zeros of the product when multiplying a number by powers of 10, and explain patterns in the placement of the decimal point when a decimal is multiplied or divided by a power of 10. Use whole-number exponents to denote powers of 10.

5.NBT.3 Read, write, and compare decimals to thousandths.

- **5.NBT.3a** Read and write decimals to thousandths using base-ten numerals, number names, and expanded form [e.g., $347.392 = 3 \times 100 + 4 \times 10 + 7 \times 1 + 3 \times (1/10) + 9 \times (1/100) + 2 \times (1/1000)$].

- **5.NBT.3b** Compare two decimals to thousandths based on meanings of the digits in each place, using >, =, and < symbols to record the results of comparisons.

5.NBT.4 Use place-value understanding to round decimals to any place.

Perform operations with multi-digit whole numbers and with decimals to hundredths.

5.NBT.5 Fluently multiply multi-digit whole numbers using the standard algorithm.

5.NBT.6 Find whole-number quotients of whole numbers with up to four-digit dividends and two-digit divisors, using strategies based on place value, the properties of operations, and/or the relationship between multiplication and division. Illustrate and explain the calculation by using equations, rectangular arrays, and/or area models.

5.NBT.7 Add, subtract, multiply, and divide decimals to hundredths, using concrete models or drawings and strategies based on place value, properties of operations, and/or the relationship between addition and subtraction; relate the strategy to a written method and explain the reasoning used.

Supporting Mathematical Thinking

A classroom culture built on caring and trust supports the intellectual growth of all students.

Creating a Classroom Culture for Success

Taking time to build a caring community in your classroom will support the intellectual growth students make, the confidence they gain, and the good mathematical thinking they do for success in school and in life. In the book *This Is Only a Test*, Nancy Litton and Maryann Wickett offer the following suggestions on building a classroom culture that promotes student success.

- **The Role of Effort and Persistence** The Standards for Mathematical Practice call for students' perseverance in solving problems. Researchers Robert Marzano, Debra Pickering, and Steven Pollock found that many students are not aware of the direct effects their efforts have on their achievement (Litton & Wickett, 2009). Teachers need to explicitly teach students about the connection between effort and achievement.
- **The Belief That Students Can and Will Make Sense of Math** Asking students to memorize procedures with little or no understanding robs them of the opportunity to make sense of math. Teachers must provide students with interesting and meaningful learning opportunities, along with the tools they need to make sense of the situation, followed by opportunities to communicate their thinking.
- **The Creation of an Environment That Encourages Risk Taking** Make it clear to students that mistakes are a natural part of learning. Establish a climate of respect among students, clearly defining what it means to critique the reasoning of others.
- **Communication and Discussion** Set an expectation that all students will actively engage in classroom discussion. Take time to purposefully teach active listening and restating someone else's thinking. Providing daily opportunities for students to talk about their ideas builds student capacity for success.
- **Partner Work and Cooperative Grouping** Researchers Robert Marzano, Debra Pickering, and Steven Pollock note that group work has a positive effect on student learning (Litton & Wickett, 2009). Provide groups with well-structured tasks that require participation by each member of the group. Make explicit connections for students between the work they do in groups and applying what they learn on independent tasks.
- **Mathematical Tools as Learning Supports** Mathematical tools should be available to students on a daily basis to use to think through and solve a problem.

Leading Meaningful Discussions

Classroom discussions are integral to effective instruction and are important vehicles for supporting students' mathematics learning.

Defining Meaningful, Productive Discussions

Through classroom discussions, students share what they know, explain their thinking, ask questions, try out new ideas, and get feedback both from the teacher and from other students in the class. Discussions give students access to mathematical ideas and give teachers access to what students understand. NCTM's *Principles and Standards* (2000) calls for incorporating communication into mathematics instruction to help students organize and consolidate their thinking, communicate coherently and clearly, analyze and evaluate the thinking and strategies of others, and use the language of mathematics.

Make sure classroom talk remains focused on important mathematics, and that students understand the role of the discussions in helping them learn the mathematics they are studying.

Establishing a Safe, Supportive Classroom Environment

Students will not engage in productive talk about mathematics if they are afraid that they will be laughed at or made to feel stupid. Teachers must be deliberate about establishing a safe and supportive environment. This can include teacher modeling by giving students time to collect their thoughts, listening attentively, being curious about their ideas, and allowing ample time for them to finish their thoughts. But it also involves being clear about expectations. It is helpful to emphasize to students that each of them has a right to be heard and an obligation to listen as they themselves will be listened to. Establish that it is okay to make mistakes, and that errors are opportunities for learning. Also, tell students that you expect them to listen to each other with respect, show patience when someone is searching for a thought, and never ridicule anyone for his or her ideas. Strategies for classroom discussions are important tools to guide students to reason about and make sense of mathematics.

Identifying Discourse Strategies

It is important to let students know that participating in class discussions is part of their responsibility as members of your class. Acknowledge that speaking to the whole class may be challenging for some, but that you expect everyone to contribute. Then provide support to help all students become better communicators.

Strategy	What It Is	How to Use It
Talk Formats	Ways teachers can configure classroom interactions for instruction	• Whole-class discussions • Small-group discussions • Partner talks
Talk Moves	Effective teacher actions to support the instructional goals of mathematical thinking and learning	• Wait Time *(Take your time to think . . . we'll wait.)* • Turn and Talk—giving students time to focus and refine their thoughts with a partner *(Think quietly for 30 seconds and then turn and share your ideas with your partner.)* • Revoicing—repeating back what a student has said to confirm what the student said was understood *(So you're saying that's an odd number?)* • Say More . . .—prompting students to expand and provide more information *(Tell us more about what you're thinking.)* • Repeating—asking students to restate someone else's reasoning *(Can you repeat what Sarah said in your own words?)* • Press for Reasoning: Why Do You Think That?—helping students provide evidence for their claims *(Why did you think that strategy would work?)* • Reasoning—asking students to apply their own reasoning to someone else's reasoning *(Do you agree or disagree and why?)* • Adding On—prompting students for further participation *(Who can add something more to this?)*

Alternative Algorithms

Algorithms are systematic, step-by-step procedures used to find the solution to a computation accurately, reliably, and efficiently.

Invented Algorithms

Some algorithms are now referred to as standard because they have been taught in the majority of US classrooms over the past 50 years. Many mathematics educators now believe it is valuable to provide frequent opportunities for students to develop, use, and discuss a variety of strategies or algorithms.

Algorithms vs. Strategies

The Common Core State Standards distinguish strategies from algorithms. An algorithm is a set of predefined steps applicable to a class of problems that gives the correct result in every case when the steps are carried out correctly. A strategy is a purposeful manipulation that may be chosen for specific problems, but may not have a fixed order, and may be aimed at converting one problem into another. An example of a strategy is computing the problem 398 + 17 by making an equivalent, but easier problem (398 + 2) + 15.

Strategies for Addition and Subtraction

The following strategies are identified in the Common Core State Standards:

- Counting on
- Making ten
- Decomposing a number leading to a ten
- Using the relationship between addition and subtraction
- Creating equivalent but easier or known sums

Reflection: Multiple Solution Strategies

1. Why is it important for the teacher and students to know multiple solution strategies?

   ____

   ____

2. How are these strategies connected to understanding our base-ten system and the properties of operations?

   ____

Analyzing Students' Thinking: Addition

Examine each solution strategy below. After analyzing the strategies, discuss the steps and what math concepts the student knew in order to use each strategy.

Kelly

$$\begin{array}{r} 567 \\ +259 \\ \hline 700 \\ 110 \\ 16 \\ \hline 826 \end{array}$$

Rudy

$$\begin{array}{r} 567 \\ +259 \\ \hline \end{array}$$

Andy

$$\begin{array}{r} 567 \\ +259 \\ \hline \end{array} \longrightarrow \begin{array}{r} 600 \\ +226 \\ \hline 826 \end{array}$$

Analyzing Students' Thinking: Subtraction

Examine each solution strategy below. After analyzing the strategies, discuss the steps and what math concepts the student knew in order to use each strategy.

Caitlin

Louis

$$\begin{array}{r} 6\not{3}^{13} \\ -\,{}^{2}\not{1}8 \\ \hline 45 \end{array}$$

Kenley

$$\begin{array}{r} 63 \\ -18 \\ \hline 28 \\ 38 \\ 48 \\ 58 \\ +\ 5 \\ \hline \end{array} \longrightarrow \left.\begin{array}{r} 10 \\ 10 \\ 10 \\ 10 \end{array}\right\} \text{or } \begin{array}{r} 40 \\ +\ 5 \\ \hline 45 \end{array}$$

Analyzing Students' Thinking: Multiplication

Examine each solution strategy below. After analyzing the strategies, discuss the steps and what math concepts the student knew in order to use each strategy.

Sasha

$$\begin{array}{r} 12 \\ \times 13 \\ \hline 6 \\ 30 \\ 20 \\ 100 \\ \hline 156 \end{array} \qquad \begin{array}{r} 43 \\ \times 62 \\ \hline 6 \\ 80 \\ 180 \\ 2400 \\ \hline 2666 \end{array}$$

Emily

$$\begin{array}{rl} 12 \times 13 & \\ 10 \times 13 = & 130 \\ 2 \times 13 = & \underline{26} \\ & 156 \end{array} \qquad \begin{array}{rl} 43 \times 62 & \\ 20 \times 62 = & 1240 \\ 20 \times 62 = & 1240 \\ 3 \times 62 = & \underline{186} \\ & 2666 \end{array}$$

125 × 36

Use both Sasha's and Emily's strategies for solving 125 × 36.

Analyzing Students' Thinking: Division

Examine each solution strategy below. After analyzing the strategies, discuss the steps and what math concepts the student knew in order to use each strategy.

689 ÷ 5 =

Use the standard algorithm for division to solve the problem above. Consider why so many students struggle with this algorithm.

Doug

137 r4	
5)689	
− 500	100 × 5
189	
50	10 × 5
139	
50	10 × 5
89	
50	10 × 5
39	
35	7 × 5
4	
	137 × 5

Madelaine

500 ÷ 5 = 100
100 ÷ 5 = 20
50 ÷ 5 = 10
30 ÷ 5 = 6
5 ÷ 5 = 1
689 ÷ 5 = 137 r4

Be ready to contribute to a discussion focused on the two questions below.

- How are these strategies different from the standard algorithm?
- How do these strategies contribute to number sense and an understanding of the operation of division?

Understanding Part-Whole Relationships

Recognizing small groups or quantities is a skill students use to develop more sophisticated understanding about number. Students first learn about part-part-whole relationships for the numbers 0 through 10.

Decomposing and Composing Numbers

Children need to develop the understanding that inside a number are other numbers. For example, they need to know that inside five is one, two, three, and four. As children grasp this understanding, they can develop the skill of flexibly decomposing numbers. This flexibility leads to the habit of looking for possible combinations that are equivalent to the number. For example, they can combine a one and a four to make five, or a two and a three.

It is important for students to have multiple opportunities to decompose the landmark numbers five and ten. They will use what they know about these smaller numbers to decompose larger numbers.

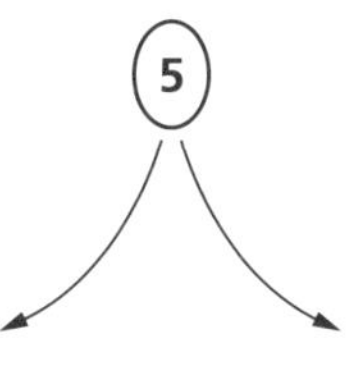

Subitizing

The identification of small quantities without counting is known as subitizing. When students are able to subitize, they are thinking of quantities as groups, rather than as individual parts of a group. This is an important step toward being able to decompose numbers.

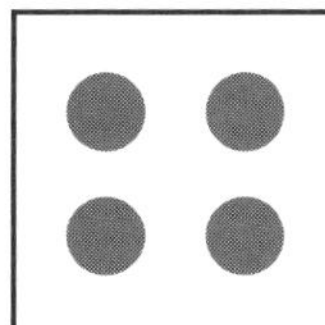

Supporting Activities

The three activities that follow provide students opportunities to see smaller numbers as parts of larger numbers. *What do you see?* offers students practice with subitizing and highlights the concept that numbers can be decomposed in different ways. One student will quickly recognize a figure of seven dots as two, three, and two, and another student sees three, three, and one. *Collect Ten* and *Sums of More Than Ten* use ten-frames to strengthen students' understanding of the landmark number of 10. In all three of these activities, students have opportunities to use equations to represent the part-whole relationships.

What Do You See?

In this routine, children are encouraged to find the smaller numbers that are part of larger numbers. They look at a card with a number of dots and describe the groups of smaller numbers that they see within the arrangement.

Key Questions

- How many dots did you see?
- How did you know there were ____?
- Who saw the dots in a different way?

Materials

- Dot cards (enlarged to $8\frac{1}{2}$ by 11 inches), 1 set
- Counters, 10 per student

Lesson Notes

1. Show a dot card to the class for about three seconds. Then, quickly hide the card.
2. Do this several times so the students figure out how many dots there are and how many smaller groupings they see there.
3. Leave the card in view. Ask the students to explain how many dots they saw and how the smaller groupings helped them remember the image. For example, a student may say, "I saw eight dots, three and three and two." Point out where those smaller groups are on the dot card.
4. On the board, label what the student saw in the form of an equation: $1 + 3 + 4 = 8$ or $8 = 3 + 3 + 2$. As you write each numeral, show the group of dots that it represents, making a clear connection between the dots and the numerals.
5. Have other students share what they saw. Each time, record what the student saw by writing an equation on the board. Encourage students to see each arrangement in various ways, to help them decompose numbers flexibly.

What Do You See? Cards

What Do You See? Cards

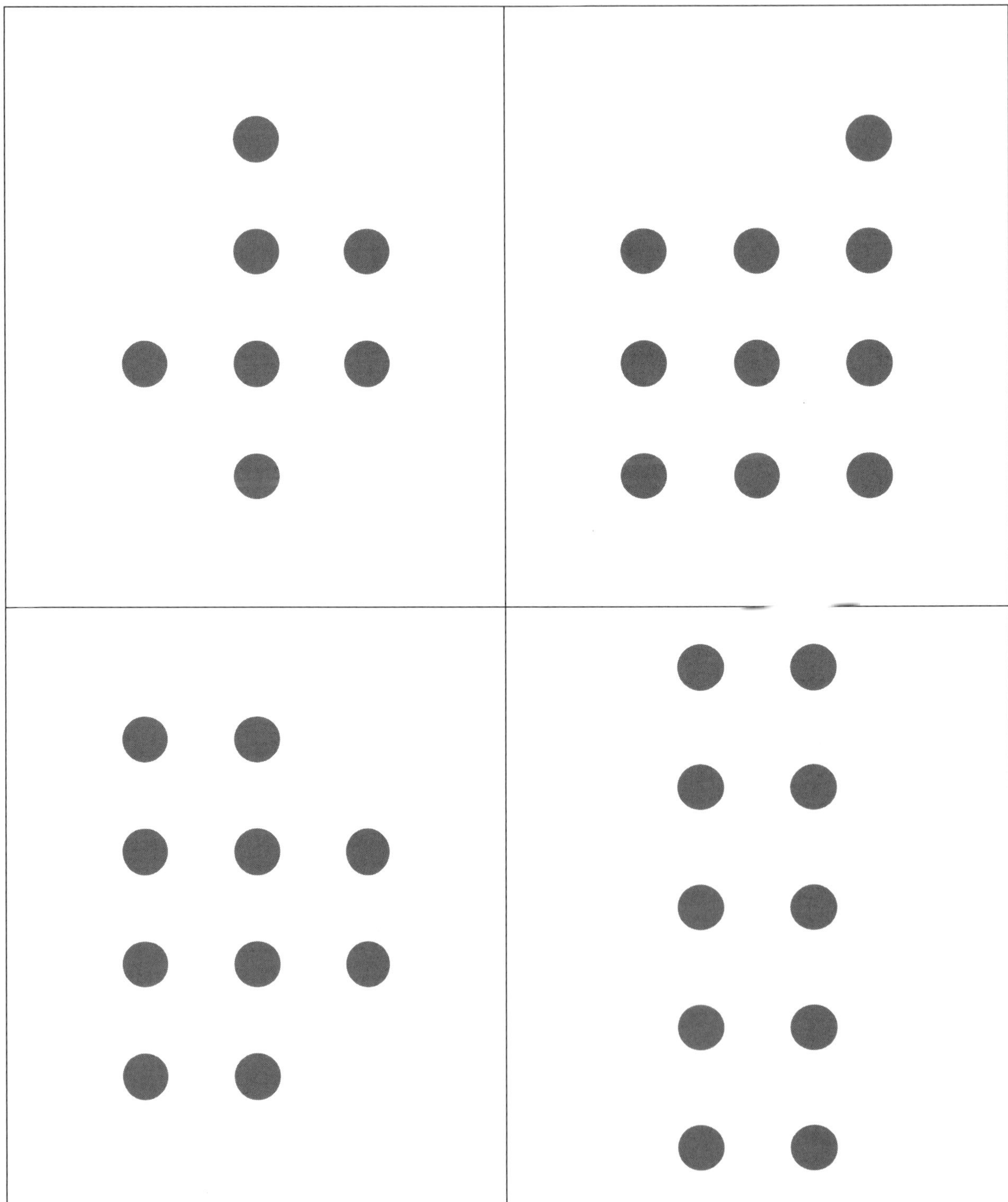

Collect Ten

In this game, students try to pair up ten-frame cards to get a sum of 10. Ten is a landmark number; by knowing combinations of 10, students can begin to construct relationships when solving other basic facts.

Key Questions

- How can you prove ____ and ____ equal 10?
- What card would you like to draw? Why?
- What are you going to ask for? Why?

Materials

- ten-frame cards, 4 sets per group of 2–4 students
- *Collect Ten* recording sheet, 1 copy per student

Introduction

1. Gather students on the floor. Select a student to model the game with you.
2. Remove the cards with 10 dots from your four sets of ten-frame cards. Deal five cards to each player. Place the rest of the cards facedown to form a deck.
3. For the model game, each player should spread their cards on the floor so all students can see them. Look for pairs of cards that have a sum of 10. Put the pairs aside.
4. Ask students, "What card do you think I should ask my partner for so that I can pair it with a card I have to make a sum of 10?" Encourage students to share their thinking with a partner. Then, call on a few volunteers to share with the class.
5. Decide what card you will ask for.
   - If your partner has the card, pair it with your card that makes a sum of 10 and set the pair of cards to the side. Your turn is over.
   - If your partner does not have the card, you must draw one card from the deck. If you can make a sum of 10, set the pair of cards to the side. If the new card does not pair with any of your cards, leave it in your hand. Your turn is over.
   - If at any point in the game you have no cards left in your hand, but cards are still available in the deck, draw two cards.
6. Tell students that it is now the other player's turn. Ask students what card they think he or she should ask for to make a sum of 10. Invite volunteers to share. Proceed with the directions described for the first player's turn.

7. Model a few more rounds. As you play, continue to verbally reinforce procedures.
8. Consider introducing the recording sheet on another day, after students are comfortable with playing *Collect Ten*.

Exploration

9. Students should play the game in small groups of two to four players.
10. The game continues until all the cards in the deck have been paired.
11. As students play, circulate and ask questions such as the key questions at the beginning of this lesson.

Summarization

12. Project a few ten-frame cards or display enlarged copies of them so that students can easily see them. Tell students that you noticed there are some sums of 10 that they know very quickly, but that they need more practice with some of them.
13. Say something like, "I would like you to explain what you do to decide what card you should ask for?"
14. Invite several students to share. If no one refers to using the ten-frame card, initiate this strategy. Point to one of the cards displayed and say something like, "This card has seven. If all the spaces were filled, it would make 10. I can count the empty spaces to find out how many more seven needs to make a sum of 10."
15. Repeat with a few more examples.

Ten-Frame Cards

Ten-Frame Cards

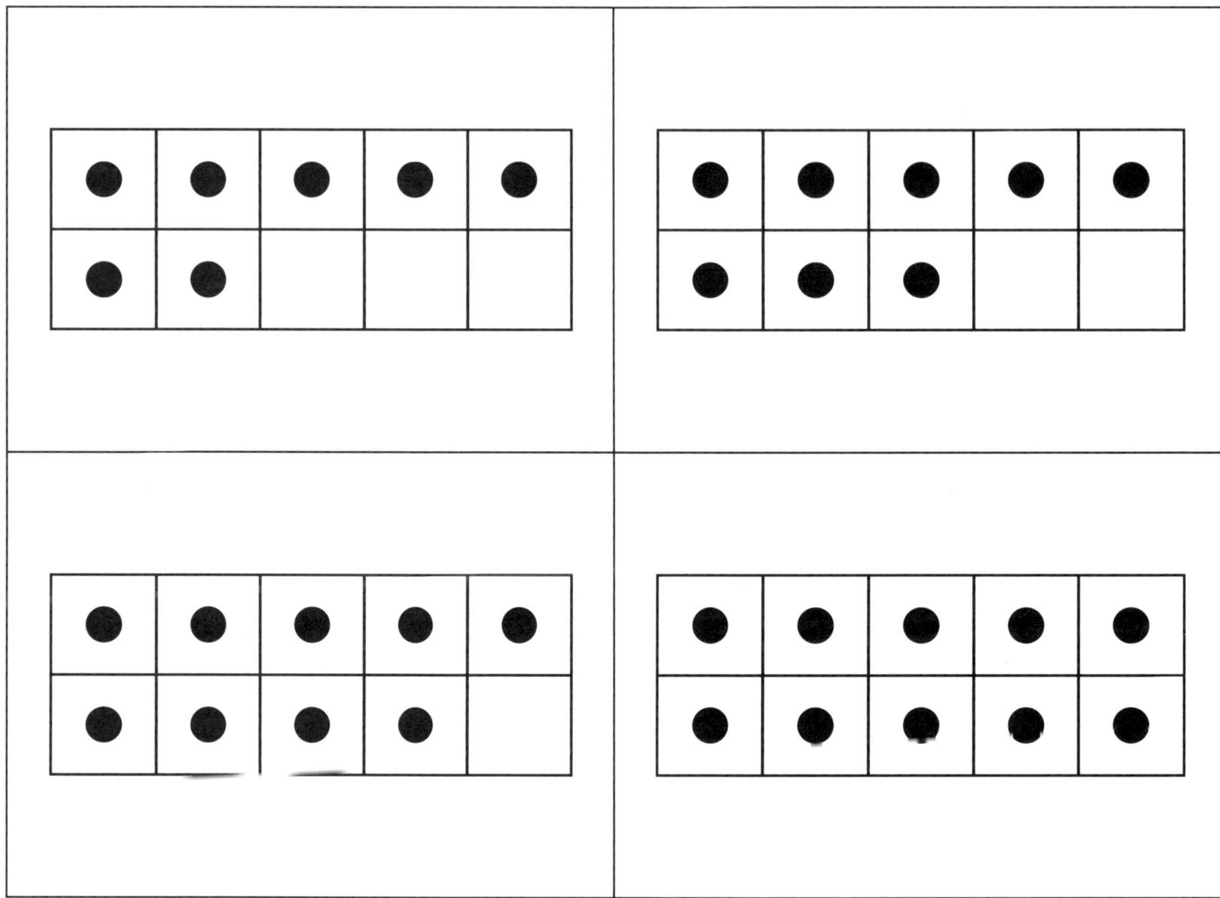

Collect Ten Recording Sheet

Name: ___________________

Directions

1. For each pair of cards you collect, write the number of the first card in the first blank, then write the number of the second card in the second blank.
2. Finally, fill in the sum in the third blank.
3. At the end of the game, complete the sentence frames at the bottom of the page.

1.	_______ + _______ = _______	**10.**	_______ + _______ = _______
2.	_______ + _______ = _______	**11.**	_______ + _______ = _______
3.	_______ + _______ = _______	**12.**	_______ + _______ = _______
4.	_______ + _______ = _______	**13.**	_______ + _______ = _______
5.	_______ + _______ = _______	**14.**	_______ + _______ = _______
6.	_______ + _______ = _______	**15.**	_______ + _______ = _______
7.	_______ + _______ = _______	**16.**	_______ + _______ = _______
8.	_______ + _______ = _______	**17.**	_______ + _______ = _______
9.	_______ + _______ = _______	**18.**	_______ + _______ = _______

My total for *Collect Ten* is __________.

My total of __________ is __________ than my partner's total of __________.

Sums of More Than Ten

This activity gives students opportunities to use and apply the strategy of making a 10 to help them solve near-10 addition facts.

Key Questions

- What combination of 10 helps you solve this problem?
- How does knowing a combination of 10 help you solve the new problem?
- How many counters do you see and how do you know?

Materials

- double ten-frame, 1 per student
- *Sums of More Than Ten* cards, 1 set per pair of students
- *Sums of More Than Ten* recording sheet, 1 per student
- counters in two colors, 10 of each color per student

Introduction

1. Place the cards in a pile upside down and turn the top card over. Build the corresponding number sentence on the demonstration double ten-frame using two colors of counters, one color for the top ten-frame and another color of counters for the bottom ten-frame. On the board, set up blanks like those seen on the recording sheet.

   ___ + ___ = ___ + ___

   ___ = ___

2. Fill in the first two blanks with the number sentence from the card you turned over.
3. Explain to students that for this activity they will need to use what they know about making 10. Ask students, "What needs to be done to make a 10?" Move the appropriate counters to make a 10 on the demonstration double ten-frame. Ask students, "What combination of 10 helps solve this problem? How many counters are left over?" Fill in the next two blanks on the board.

   7 + 5 = ___ + ___

   ___ = ___

4. Ask students to think about what they see on the demonstration double ten-frame. What is the total number of counters? Record the sum for each side of the equation.

   7 + 5 = **10 + 2**

   ___ = ___

5. Tell students they will turn over the next *Sums of More Than Ten* card and build the number sentence on their double ten-frame, then record it on their copy of the *Sums of More Than Ten* recording sheet. They will work to make a 10 and record a number sentence to match their thinking. Finally, they will record the sum.

7 + 5 = 10 + 2

12 = 12

Exploration

6. Pass out the *Sums of More Than Ten* cards and recording sheets. Make sure each student (or pair of students) has 10 counters of one color and 10 counters of another color. If you choose to let students work in pairs, explain that each student will write on his or her own recording sheet but will share a double ten-frame, counters, and a set of *Sums of More Than Ten* cards with a partner. Model one round with a partner so students understand how to work together.

7. As students work, circulate and observe how they model problems on the double ten-frame and how they record their work. Ask questions to encourage them to think about the mathematics and to help you assess their depth of understanding.
   - Tell me how the counters on your ten-frame represent the problem?
   - What will the equation be after you make a 10? Can you prove that?

Summarization

8. Gather students for a discussion. During the discussion, reinforce the idea of making a 10 and making a connection between the concrete representation of the counters and abstract representation of the equations. Project a double ten-frame on a whiteboard or use magnets on a metal cookie sheet so that all students can see the model.

9. Draw a card and ask a volunteer to represent the problem with counters on the ten-frame. To keep other students engaged, ask them to close their eyes and visualize what the counters will look like. Then, they can open their eyes and compare to what they see on the double ten-frame. Ask questions such as the following:
   - I see xx counters on the top ten-frame. How many more do we need to make a 10?
   - After we make a 10, what will we see on the double ten-frame? How can we represent that with an equation?
   - Why do you think it is a good strategy to look for ways to make a 10?

Sums of More Than Ten Cards, Version 1

7 + 5 =	5 + 6 =
4 + 8 =	8 + 7 =
9 + 3 =	9 + 7 =
7 + 4 =	6 + 7 =
9 + 6 =	8 + 5 =

Sums of More Than Ten Cards, Version 2

8 + 3 =	5 + 8 =
4 + 9 =	9 + 5 =
7 + 8 =	9 + 7 =
5 + 7 =	4 + 7 =
8 + 9 =	6 + 5 =

Sums of More Than Ten Recording Sheet

Name: ____________________

Directions

1. Turn over the top *Sums of More Than Ten* card in your pile and record the number sentence.
2. Use counters to build the number sentence on your double ten-frame.
3. Make a 10 by rearranging the counters you've placed and record the new number sentence.
4. Figure out the sum. Record the sum for both sentences.

1. __________ + __________ = __________ + __________

__________ = __________

2. __________ + __________ = __________ + __________

__________ = __________

3. __________ + __________ = __________ + __________

__________ = __________

4. __________ + __________ = __________ + __________

__________ = __________

(continued)

Sums of More Than Ten Recording Sheet *(continued)*

5. __________ + __________ = __________ + __________

__________ = __________

6. __________ + __________ = __________ + __________

__________ = __________

7. __________ + __________ = __________ + __________

__________ = __________

8. __________ + __________ = __________ + __________

__________ = __________

9. __________ + __________ = __________ + __________

__________ = __________

10. __________ + __________ = __________ + __________

__________ = __________

Spill and Compare

This lesson encourages children to compare numbers, record and interpret tallies, and consider odd and even numbers.

Key Questions

- Which is more, the red or the yellow?
- Which section has more tallies?
- Do all numbers have tallies in the box for same number of red and yellow? Why?

Materials
• two-color counters, 6 per pair of students
• paper, 1 per pair of students
• *Spill and Compare* recording sheet, 1 per pair of students

Introduction

1. Ask a student to be your partner to demonstrate the game using the target number six. Have a recording sheet available to model recording during the activity.
2. Cup six counters in your hands, and spill them onto the paper workspace. Ask students whether more reds, more yellows, or the same number of reds and yellows came up. Count the red counters and then the yellow counters to check.
3. Show the children the recording sheet. Make a tally under the section corresponding with the configuration of colors that was thrown. Remind the children how to make tally marks in groups of five.
4. Spill, compare, and record the counters several times.

Exploration

5. Ask the students to spill and record, taking turns with their partner, until the recording sheet shows 20 tallies.
6. Give partners six counters and a recording sheet to share. Have them work together, taking turns shaking and spilling the counters and recording their data.

Summarization

7. Gather the students on the rug to interpret the data from several of their recording sheets. Reproduce a sample recording sheet on the chalkboard, using a pair of students' data. For example, the board might look like this:

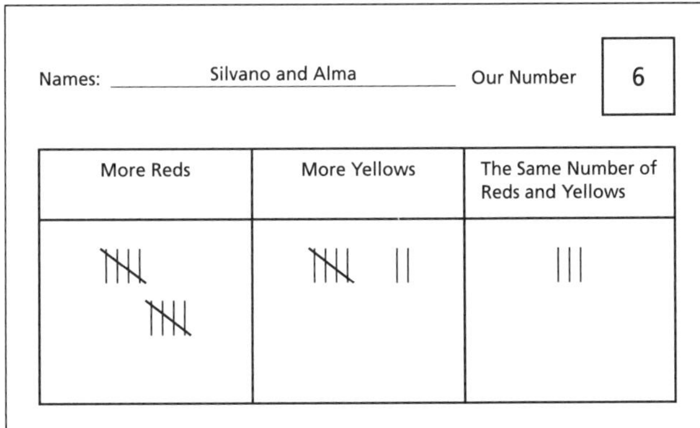
Names: Silvano and Alma Our Number 6

More Reds	More Yellows	The Same Number of Reds and Yellows

8. Have the class interpret the information on the board. Ask students to practice reading the tallies and explaining how they knew the number of tallies. Some children will count all the tallies. Others will figure out the number without having to count every single tally.
9. For each section on the sample chart, record the total number. Then examine the chart to see which section had more: More Reds, More Yellows, or The Same Number of Reds and Yellows. Put a star next to the section with the most tallies.
10. Do the same with another recording sheet to give the students practice interpreting tally marks. Ask, "Is there a way to know how many tallies there are without counting each one?"

Extension: Investigating New Numbers and Odd and Even

1. Before the lesson, prepare index cards labeled 2 through 12. One card is needed for each pair of students. It is possible that duplicate numbers may be needed.
2. Remind students how they previously spilled the counters and filled in their charts. Explain that they will do the same thing today,

Materials

- two-color counters, 12 per pair of students
- *Spill and Compare* recording sheet, 1 per pair of students and a few extras
- index cards, each labeled with one number from 2–12 with duplicate cards for 6–10, 1 set for the class
- chart with numbers 2–12
- 1 red marker and 1 yellow marker

but that they will choose their own number card, picking a number to explore. Remind the students that they will again shake and spill 20 times. Then, they will determine the number of tallies in each section, and put a star in the section that receives the most tallies.

3. When partners complete a recording sheet for one number, they can choose a new number to explore. Save all recording sheets until you are ready to facilitate a discussion about odd and even numbers.
4. Gather students on the rug with their previously completed recording sheets. Focus students' attention on the last section of each recording sheet. Ask students that investigated the number two whether they had any tallies in the box for Same Number of Reds and Yellows. Write yes on the poster if the number 2 does have tallies in that section, and write no if there are no tallies there.
5. Continue doing this, in order, for each number on the poster. Ask students what patterns they notice.
6. Distribute 12 counters to each pair of students. They should use the counters to show how the counters looked to have the same number of reds as yellows. Direct students to start with the number 2. When students share, record 1+1 next to the 2 on the chart. Then, draw one red circle and one yellow circle next to the equation.
7. Direct students to repeat this for three counters. When students agree that it is impossible to have the same number of reds and yellows, ask them to try it for the number four.
8. As you facilitate this investigation and discussion with the other numbers, encourage students to make predictions and explain what they notice. Some students are likely to initiate the idea that some numbers have uneven rows of yellow and red or that with some numbers you can't make partners. When the majority of students are discussing and noticing this idea, say something like, "Eight is an even number. Can you see why we say even?"
9. Ask the students whether nine is even. When students explain that it is not, introduce the vocabulary word *odd*.
10. When the chart is complete, ask multiple students to explain what even numbers are.

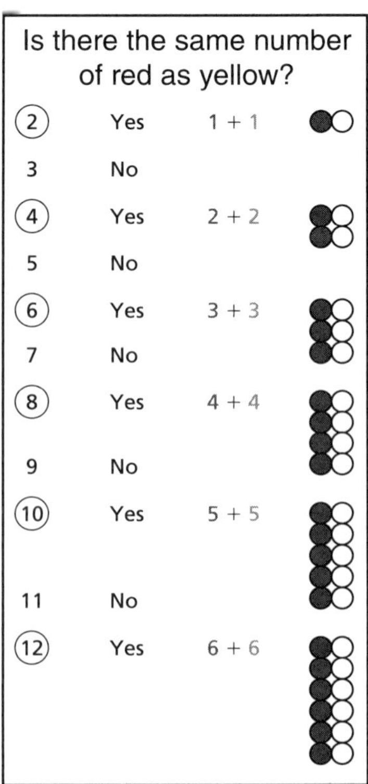

Is there the same number of red as yellow?

(2)	Yes	1 + 1
3	No	
(4)	Yes	2 + 2
5	No	
(6)	Yes	3 + 3
7	No	
(8)	Yes	4 + 4
9	No	
(10)	Yes	5 + 5
11	No	
(12)	Yes	6 + 6

Spill and Compare Recording Sheet

Names: ______________________ Our Number ☐

More Reds	More Yellows	The Same Number of Reds and Yellows

Names: ______________________ Our Number ☐

More Reds	More Yellows	The Same Number of Reds and Yellows

Hundred Chart

The hundred chart is a valuable tool that helps children build a mental model of the mathematical structure of our base-ten number system. Hundred charts allow children to explore concepts from counting to adding two-digit numbers.

Scribing Student Strategies

Students often struggle with what to write on paper to represent their thinking. It is helpful for them to see how the teacher records their strategies. Drawings of a partial hundred chart, open number line, or an illustration of hands (if the student counted on her fingers) are all direct representations of how students may think.

How many more do you need to get from 45 to 100?

Student 1 responds, "I put my finger on 45 and counted by tens to 95, and then I counted by ones over to 100. So I said 10, 20, 30, 40, 50, 51, 52, 53, 54, 55. I know I need 55 to reach 100."

Teacher records,

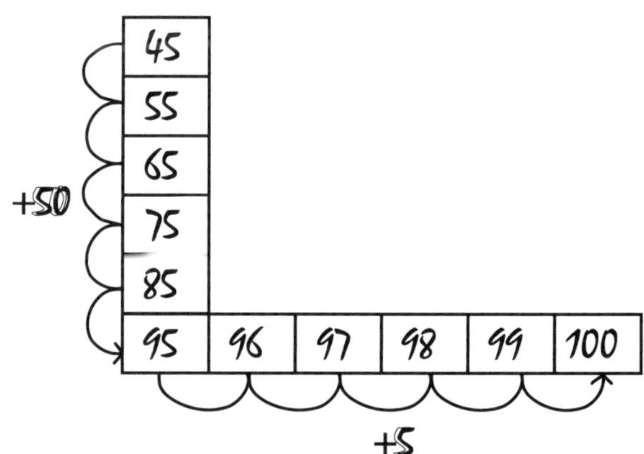

Teacher says, "I drew a partial hundreds chart to show what you did. Another way we can record your thinking is with an equation. You said you started on 45 and added 50, so I'll record 45 plus 50 equals 95. Then you said you added five more, so I'll record 95 plus five equals 100. You looked at what you added and it was 55."

$45 + 50 = 95$

$95 + 5 = 100$

55

Student 2 responds, "I did it in my brain. I counted to 95. I said 55, 65, 75, 85, 95, and saw I had five fingers up and that's 50 since I was counting by tens. Then I knew I needed five more to get to 100; 50 and five is 55."

Teacher records,

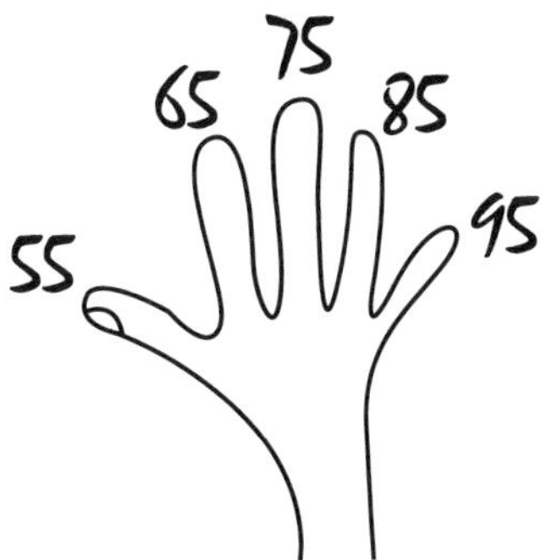

Teacher says, "You used your fingers to keep track of your counting, which is helpful. We can also record your thinking with an equation."

$$45 + 50 = 95$$
$$95 + 5 = 100$$

55

Scribing With the Open Number Line

How far is it from 42 to 100?

Student 1 says, "I put my finger on 42 and counted over to 50, which was eight. Then I added tens until I landed on 100. I added five tens. 50 and eight is 58."

Student 2 says, "I counted by tens from 42. So I went 52, 62, 72, 82, 92, which was 50, and then I counted over from 92, which was 58."

+10 +10 +10 +10 +10 +8

42 52 62 72 82 92 93 94 95 96 97 98 99 100

Hundred Chart Puzzle

Varied and repeated experiences are needed to help students create a mental image of the hundred chart. The puzzles students create in this lesson can be used again in a center.

Key Questions

- Where does this piece belong on the hundred chart?
- How do you know it fits there?
- What number will be above (or below) ____?
- What patterns help you know where numbers go?

Materials

- 10-by-10 grid, 1 per student and a few extras
- letter-size envelope, 1 per student
- 100 chart wall chart
- 9 small sticky notes

Lesson Notes

Prior to the lesson, prepare the hundred wall chart by covering selected numbers with sticky notes. Cover two sets of numbers; one in the shape of a square, and on a different part of the chart, five numbers in the shape of a Z.

Introduction

1. Focus students' attention on the four numbers, in the shape of a square, that are covered on the chart. Ask students to share ideas for how we know what numbers are hidden. After hearing several ideas, remove the sticky notes to verify predictions. Repeat this process with the other set of hidden numbers.

Exploration

2. Distribute the 10-by-10 grids and direct students to write the numbers from 1 to 100.
3. Explain the parameters of cutting puzzle pieces. Each piece should have between 7 and 12 numbers. Cuts are only made on the lines. Students need to write their name or initials on the back of each piece.

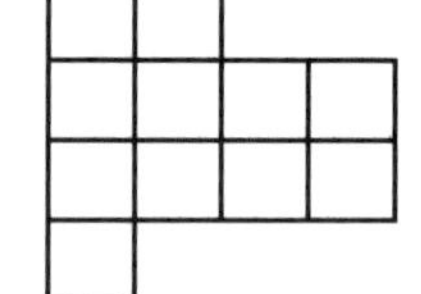

4. Direct students to put their puzzles back together after cutting out the pieces. Then, they should write their name on an envelope and store the pieces inside. With remaining time, they can trade puzzles with each other to solve a new puzzle. Direct them to sign their name on the back of an envelope when they solve that puzzle.

Summarization

5. Gather students in a circle on the floor. Draw multiple sample puzzle pieces on the board and write one number in each piece. Engage students in discussing how to determine the other numbers on the puzzle piece.

10-by-10 Grid

Hippety Hop

During this game, students use hops of one, 10, or 100 to reach a target number on the hundred chart. The game increases students' understanding of number relations and develops computational fluency.

Key Questions

- Why did you choose the set of hops that you did?
- Why might you sometimes go past the target number while hopping?

Materials
• pocket hundred chart with removable number cards or poster of hundred chart
• 100 chart, 1 per pair of students
• paper, 1 sheet per pair of students

Introduction

1. Gather students where everyone can see a displayed hundred chart. Explain *Hippety Hop* to the students. Tell them they will be given a target number to reach by making hops of one, 10, or 100. They may add or subtract to move to the target number. The object of the game is to get to the target number in the fewest hops.
2. Model one round for the students by writing the target number 18 for all to see. Explain the various ways to "hop":

   "I can hop to 18 by making 18 hops of one." Move your finger one number at a time from 1 to 18, then record 1 + 1 + 1 + 1 + 1 + 1 + 1 + 1 + 1 + 1 + 1 + 1 + 1 + 1 + 1 + 1 + 1 + 1.

   "Or I can hop to 18 by making some hops of tens and ones. I'll hop to 10 and 20, and then back two ones." Move your finger to 10, 20, 19, 18, and record 10 + 10 − 1 − 1 = 18.

   "Or I can hop to 18 by making a hop of 10 and some hops of ones. I'll hop to 10 and then make eight hops of one to 18." Move your finger to 10, 11, 12, 13, 14, 15, 16, 17, 18, and record 10 + 1 + 1 + 1 + 1 + 1 + 1 + 1 + 1 = 18.
3. Emphasize to students that each number, whether it's a plus or a minus, represents a hop. Point to +10 and ask, "What does this plus 10 represent?" Repeat this questioning procedure with +1 and −1.

4. Point to the first equation and ask the class to count the hops with you as you point to each +1. Record 18 hops next to the equation. Point to the second equation and ask the class to count the hops with you as you point to 10 + 10 − 1 − 1. Record four hops next to the equation. Point to the third equation and ask the class to count the hops with you as you point to 10 + 1 + 1 + 1 + 1 + 1 + 1 + 1 + 1. Record nine hops next to the equation. Ask, "Which equation gets us to our target number in the fewest hops?" Circle or star the correct equation.

5. Model another round with the students, but this time elicit their thinking. Write the target number 74 where everyone can see it. Tell the class you would like to start off by modeling one way to hop to 74. Move your finger to 100, 90, 80, 70, 71, 72, 73, 74.

   Say, "Can someone describe the hops I just made?" As a student revoices your moves, record 100 − 10 − 10 − 10 + 1 + 1 + 1 + 1 = 74.

6. Ask students to think about how they would like to hop to 74 using one, 10, or 100. Give them a few moments to think, and then ask them to turn to their partner to explain how they would hop to 74.

7. Call on a few students to explain how they would hop to 74. Have them come up to the class hundreds chart to show their hops. When a student is finished, call on another student to revoice the hops. Record the hops using equations.

8. When a few equations have been recorded, ask the class to count the hops with you by counting the addends in each equation. Record the number of hops next to the equations and discuss which equation used the fewest hops. Circle or star the equation with the fewest hops.

Exploration

9. Tell students they will work with a partner and hop to the target numbers, trying to make the fewest hops possible. Explain that, just like when you played the game together as a class, they will write the equations and then count the hops.

10. Model another round with the class and allow students to ask questions if they need clarification.

11. Pair up students and pass out one sheet of paper and one hundred chart per pair. Record the following target numbers for all to see: 16, 33, 78, 82 and 55.

12. Observe students as they work. Engage them in conversation and ask the key questions listed at the beginning of the game.

Summarization

13. Ask students to review their equations. Then begin a class discussion to find the fewest hops for each number. Record only for equations with the fewest hops for each number.

    Ask, "When is it most helpful to hop to 100? Why? When is it most helpful to hop past the target number? Why?"

QuietWrite

1. ***How do you think the hundred chart could be a valuable tool for your students?***

Hundred Chart

1	2	3	4	5	6	7	8	9	10
11	12	13	14	15	16	17	18	19	20
21	22	23	24	25	26	27	28	29	30
31	32	33	34	35	36	37	38	39	40
41	42	43	44	45	46	47	48	49	50
51	52	53	54	55	56	57	58	59	60
61	62	63	64	65	66	67	68	69	70
71	72	73	74	75	76	77	78	79	80
81	82	83	84	85	86	87	88	89	90
91	92	93	94	95	96	97	98	99	100

Look, Quick!

This lesson develops students' ability to see and recognize groups of numbers instead of always counting by ones. The ability to see groups of objects is known as subitizing.

Key Questions

- How many squares are colored in? How do you know?

Lesson Notes

1. Gather students in a whole-group area and display a 10-by-10 grid. Count the rows and columns with students to determine the total number of squares on the grid.
2. Explain that you will color in some rows and a few leftover squares. Tell students they need to determine how many squares have been colored in, but they can only see the grid for a few seconds. Explain that you will mark the chart to show some benchmark numbers that will help them quickly see how much is colored in.
3. Count over five squares and draw a vertical line down the grid.
4. Next, color in 15 squares (the top row and the first five squares on the second row), but don't let students watch as you do this.
5. Show the grid to the class for modeling purposes only; allow them to see it for as long as necessary. Ask, "How does the dark line help you see what's been colored in?"
6. Now color in 25 squares (the first two top rows and the first five squares on the third row). Once again, do not let students see you doing this!
7. Show the grid to the class and ask, "How does the dark line help you see what's been colored in?"
8. Explain that we have a benchmark for fives and you would like to add a benchmark for 50. Count by tens until you reach the 50th square and draw a horizontal black line.

9. Now color in 70 and ask, "How does the dark line help you see what's been colored in?"
10. Remind students that you will color in some squares and they will be given a few seconds to determine how many squares are colored in. Encourage them to use the benchmarks of five and 50.
11. Start with simple numbers like 15, 35, 40, and 60 so students can become familiar with the format of having to look quickly, and can also begin using the benchmarks. After each number is shown, ask students the key questions, "How many squares are colored in? How do you know?"
12. Move on to more complex numbers. Color in 33 squares, show the class, and ask for volunteers to share how many squares they believe are colored in. Encourage them to explain how they knew what was colored in, and you record their thinking using equations.

Examples of Student Thinking and Teacher Recording

Student says: "I knew the first three rows is 30 and then I counted by ones: 31, 32, 33."

Teacher records: 30 + 1 + 1 + 1 = 33

Student says: "I saw 30. Then I saw it was almost to the five line but it was two away so that's three. Thirty and three is 33."

Teacher records: 30 + (5 – 2) = 33 or 30 + 3 = 33

13. Continue coloring more complex numbers and connecting student thinking to the matching equations.
14. After several sessions of Look, Quick!, ask students to explain how the benchmark numbers of five and 50 help them see quickly how many squares are colored in.

Race to 100

During the game, students add or subtract five, 10, or multiples of 10 as they try to reach or go over 100 before their partner. Students answer questions that give them an opportunity to think more about number relationships.

Key Questions

- How did you solve what was asked of you on the action card?
- How did you solve what was asked of you on the question card?
- How can you make the number on the action card with the fives and tens strips?

Materials
• hundred chart, 1 per student • Fives Strips, 1 cut set per pair of students • Tens Strips, 1 cut set per pair of students • Action Cards, 1 cut set per pair of students • Question Cards, 1 cut set per pair of students

Introduction

1. Gather students in a circle and place the materials in the middle of the circle so all students can see them.
2. Tell students they are going to learn to play *Race to 100.* The objective of the game is to get to or go over 100 before your opponent. To play, you draw an action card, perform the action by placing the appropriate strips on a hundred chart, and then draw a question card and answer the question. Play continues until someone gets to or goes over 100.
3. Model for students how to shuffle the action cards and place them in a pile. Do the same with the question cards and place them in another pile.
4. Select a student to play against you. Place a hundred chart in front of the student and one in front of you. Place the fives and tens strips in the middle so that you can both reach them. Explain to students they will draw an action card and find the appropriate strips to place on the hundred chart. If they draw a minus card in the first round, they need to place it in the middle of the action card pile and draw again. Model the first round for them. The following is a sample teacher explanation: "I drew a plus 20 action card from the pile. This means I need to add 20, or cover 20 spaces on the hundred chart. I can make 20 using two tens strips because 10 plus 10 is 20. I could also use four fives strips because five plus five plus five plus five is 20. I'm going to choose to cover 20 spaces with two tens strips."

5. Next, draw a question card and read the card aloud to the class. The question card is: *What is 10 more than what you have right now?* Pause for a few moments to give students time to think about the answer. Ask them to whisper the answer to a partner and then raise their hand if they are willing to share their thinking.
6. After you have completed your round with the students, model placing the action card into one discard pile and the question card into another discard pile. Ask the student to go next.
7. For your next turn, tell the class you are going to purposefully find the −5 action card so they can have a discussion about it.
8. Point to the two tens strips and explain that you will need to trade for some five strips because you don't have a fives strip to take away. Pick up one tens strip, lay it to the side, and then place two fives strips under it so students can see they are equal. Explain the trade to students before putting the two fives strips on the hundred chart.
9. Next, remind students that they need to take five away (per the action card). Pick up the fives strip from the hundred chart. Ask students, "What is twenty minus five?"
10. Then, draw a question card and read the card aloud to the class. The question card is: *How many more do you need to reach 100?* Pause for a few moments to give students time to think about the answer. Ask them to whisper to a partner and then raise their hand if they are willing to share their thinking.
11. Finish a complete game with students so game scenarios can be discussed before students play with a partner.

Exploration

12. Put students into pairs. Give each pair two copies of the hundred charts, a set of action and question cards, and fives and tens strips.
13. Observe as partners play. Assist when needed, and ask the key questions listed at the beginning of the game.

Summarization

14. After students have had time to play the game, begin a class discussion with the purpose of linking their thinking to the symbols.
15. Display a hundred chart with 45 spaces covered. Ask the following questions from the question card pile: *How many more do you need to reach 100?* Ask students to think quietly for a moment about the question and then share their thoughts with a partner.
16. As students share their thinking, record it symbolically. See page 54 for recording examples.
17. Acknowledge the different ways of thinking about the same problem. Ask students to look for similarities in the different methods. Also, discuss the various ways to record student thinking.

Race to 100 Fives Strips

5	5
5	5
5	5
5	5
5	5

Race to 100 Tens Strips

10

10

10

10

10

10

10

Race to 100 Action Cards

+10	+10	+10
+10	+10	+20
+20	+20	+30
+30	+5	+5
−10	−10	−10
−20	−5	−5

Race to 100 Question Cards

How many more do you need to reach 100?	How many more do you need to reach 100?	How many more do you need to reach 100?
How far from 50 are you?	How far from 50 are you?	How far from 50 are you?
What is 10 *more* than what you have right now?	What is 10 *more* than what you have right now?	What is 10 *more* than what you have right now?
What is 10 *less* than what you have right now?	What is 10 *less* than what you have right now?	What is 10 *less* than what you have right now?
What is 5 *more* than what you have right now?	What is 5 *more* than what you have right now?	What is 5 *more* than what you have right now?
What is 5 *less* than what you have right now?	What is 5 *less* than what you have right now?	What is 5 *less* than what you have right now?

How Far Away?

In this game, students use the landmark number of 100 to explore other numbers and their relationships to one hundred. They gain valuable experience connecting subtraction and addition.

Key Questions

- How far from 100 is the number? How do you know?
- What is similar about the strategies? What is different?
- Would you rather add up from the number or subtract from 100? Why?

Materials

- dice, 3 per pair of students
- hundred chart, 1 per pair of students
- counters, 6 per pair of students
- pocket hundred chart or projected hundred chart

Introduction

1. Introduce the game. Explain to students that they will roll three dice, create two-digit numbers, and figure out how far from 100 a few of the numbers are.
2. Distribute copies of the hundred chart, one to each pair of students.
3. Roll the three dice and record the numbers on the board. Ask students to work with a partner and determine several two-digit numbers that can be created from the numbers rolled.
4. As volunteers share numbers, mark the numbers on the pocket wall chart. Select one of the numbers and tell students you want them to find the difference between that number and 100. They will determine how far it is from ____ to 100. Ask students to talk with their partner and determine the difference.
5. Call on volunteers to share their strategies. Use an open number line to record their thinking. (For examples of recording on an open number line, see page 55.)
6. Select another number that is marked on the hundred chart and ask students to find the difference from 100. Scribe students' strategies again.

Exploration

7. Review your expectations with students. They should roll three dice. Create several two-digit numbers and mark them on the hundred chart with counters. They choose two numbers and find the difference between the numbers and 100. They need to record their strategies using equations, open number lines, or partial drawings of the hundred chart.
8. As students work, walk from group to group, asking the key questions listed at the beginning of the lesson.

Summarization

9. Gather students for a whole-class discussion. Select a number marked on the hundred chart from the introduction of the game, and ask students to find the difference.
10. Call on a volunteer and scribe his or her thinking. If the student uses addition, say something like, "This strategy is called adding on or finding the missing addend." Model for students how to record with a missing addend. 31 + _____ = 100
11. Encourage students to think about how to record the same problem as a subtraction problem. (100 − _____ = 31) Tell students this is called subtracting from or finding the missing number.
12. Scribe other strategies. Encourage students to discuss what is similar and what is different.

Guess My Number

Guess My Number **develops students' number sense by giving them opportunities to think about the relationships between and among numbers and by helping them gain an understanding of the relative position and magnitude of whole numbers.**

Key Questions

- I'm thinking of a number between ____ and ____. What is your guess?
- What numbers are good guesses? Why?
- What do you know about my number?

Materials

- 2 sticky notes, 1 with a left-facing arrow and 1 with a right-facing arrow

Lesson Notes (Kindergarten–Grade 1)

1. Draw a number line on the board.

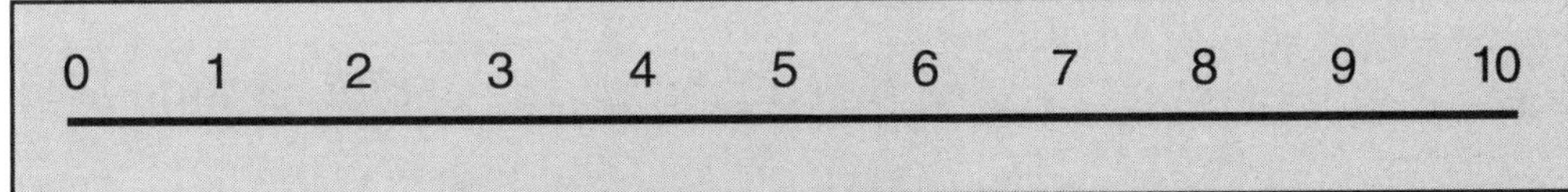

2. For a warm-up, point to different numbers and ask students to say the name of the number and show you that amount with their fingers. Then, explain to students you have picked a secret number and they will try to guess it.
3. Have individual students guess your secret number; if the guess is incorrect, announce whether your number is greater or less than the number suggested. For Grades K–1, use sticky notes with left- and right-facing arrows on them to help students see how their guesses continue to narrow the options for the secret number.
4. Call on a volunteer. After he or she makes a guess, tell the class whether your number is more or less than that guess. Use a sticky note arrow on the number line as a reminder of the feedback.
5. Continue responding to guesses and moving the arrow(s) on the number line to reflect new information. Ask students to share which numbers are good guesses.

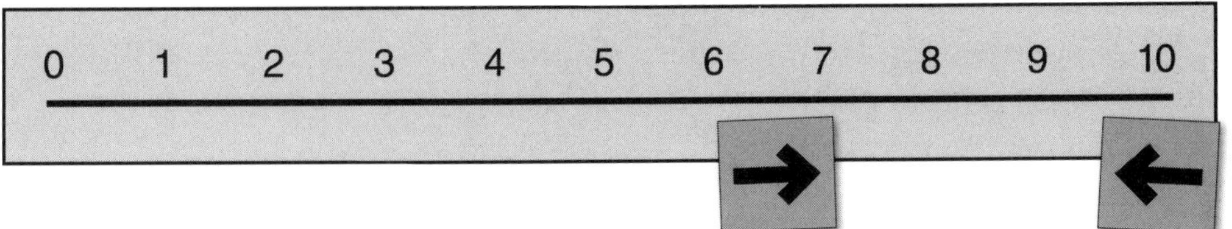

6. Continue until someone guesses your secret number.

Lesson Notes (Grade 2)

1. Draw the range of a number line on the board and mark an X where your secret number is.

2. Ask, "Is my number less or greater than 10?" After hearing students' responses, add 10 to the number line and ask students to talk with a partner about what the secret number is.
3. Listen to students' guesses and then elicit their help in determining where to put 25.
4. Ask students if they want to revise guesses. Then, reveal your secret number to the class.

Be ready to contribute to a discussion focused on the two questions below.

- How do you think the activity *Guess My Number* and the practice page will support students making sense of the open number line?
- Why is it important to make connections with the hundred chart?

Scaffolding the Open Number Line

The open number line is a computational tool for addition and subtraction that provides students with a visual model that is useful for building understanding and skills.

Explicit Instruction

Some students may need explicit instruction helping them build on their prior experience with the hundred chart.

What does the ___ stand for?

What does the + ___ stand for?

What does the ___ stand for?

I collected ___ acorns.

Then I collected ____ more.

How many acorns do I have?

1–100 Chart

1	2	3	4	5	6	7	8	9	10
11	12	13	14	15	16	17	18	19	20
21	22	23	24	25	26	27	28	29	30
31	32	33	34	35	36	37	38	39	40
41	42	43	44	45	46	47	48	49	50
51	52	53	54	55	56	57	58	59	60
61	62	63	64	65	66	67	68	69	70
71	72	73	74	75	76	77	78	79	80
81	82	83	84	85	86	87	88	89	90
91	92	93	94	95	96	97	98	99	100

Open Number Line
Equation

Scaffolding the Open Number Line

(continued)

I picked ___ apples.

Then I picked ____ more.

How many apples do I have?

1–100 Chart

1	2	3	4	5	6	7	8	9	10
11	12	13	14	15	16	17	18	19	20
21	22	23	24	25	26	27	28	29	30
31	32	33	34	35	36	37	38	39	40
41	42	43	44	45	46	47	48	49	50
51	52	53	54	55	56	57	58	59	60
61	62	63	64	65	66	67	68	69	70
71	72	73	74	75	76	77	78	79	80
81	82	83	84	85	86	87	88	89	90
91	92	93	94	95	96	97	98	99	100

Open Number Line

Equation

1–100 Chart

1	2	3	4	5	6	7	8	9	10
11	12	13	14	15	16	17	18	19	20
21	22	23	24	25	26	27	28	29	30
31	32	33	34	35	36	37	38	39	40
41	42	43	44	45	46	47	48	49	50
51	52	53	54	55	56	57	58	59	60
61	62	63	64	65	66	67	68	69	70
71	72	73	74	75	76	77	78	79	80
81	82	83	84	85	86	87	88	89	90
91	92	93	94	95	96	97	98	99	100

Open Number Line

Equation

101 and Out

This game involves addition as well as place value. It gives students an opportunity to think strategically while working with the concepts of tens and ones.

Key Questions:

- Will you place the number in the ones place or the tens place? Why?
- What do you hope to roll next? Why?
- If you rolled a 2 on your first roll, where might you place it and why?

Materials
• dice, 1 per pair of students • hundred chart, 1 per pair of students • counters, 1 per student • *101 and Out* Recording Sheet, 1 per student

Introduction

1. Gather students and introduce *101 and Out.* Tell students they will roll one die, decide whether the number should be placed in the ones place or the tens place, and repeat this five more times. The objective is to get as close to 100 as you can without going over.
2. Choose a student to model the game with you and display two copies of the hundred charts, one for you and one for the student.
3. Model rolling the die. Share your thinking aloud to help students understand the concept of the game. For example, "I rolled a five. I can place the five in the ones place so the value is five, or I can place the five in the tens place so the value is 50. I am going to choose 50 and put my counter on 50 and record 50 on the recording sheet."
4. On chart paper or the board, record the open number line illustration that represents that turn.
5. Player 2 takes his or her turn, repeating everything from steps 3 and 4.
6. Players repeat steps, this time adding the newly created number to the number from round 1.
7. Play continues until both players have rolled the die six times. Then, players compare their totals to see who is closer to 100 without going over.

Exploration

8. Post a reminder of the rules so that students have a reference.

Game Directions

1. Roll the die.
2. Create a number.
3. Move your counter on the hundred chart.
4. Record the number on the recording sheet.
5. Find the sum.
6. Pass the die to your partner.

9. Distribute two recording sheets, one hundred chart, two counters, and one die per pair of students. As students play, circulate, asking the key questions listed at the beginning of the game.

Summarization

10. Display a partially completed recording sheet that indicates that after three turns, a player is on the number 55. Tell students that the next number rolled is a 3. Ask them to think first and then talk with a partner about what they would do.
11. After a couple of minutes, invite volunteers to share. Come to a final class agreement, and mark the recording sheet accordingly.
12. Tell students the next number rolled is a 1. Repeat the previous discussion. Would they put the 1 in the ones or tens place and why?
13. After several students share their thinking, come to a final class agreement and mark the recording sheet.
14. Ask students to think quietly by themselves about which number they would hope to roll next. Give them an opportunity to share with a partner and then invite volunteers to discuss their thinking.

101 and Out Recording Sheet

The game and recording method are modeled in this session. Note that the first example of "Equation" below starts on 1 because players start with 1 on the hundred chart used in this game.

Players take turns for up to six rolls each.

1. Roll the cube and record it.
2. Decide whether to use the roll as tens or ones. Add with an open number line.
3. Write an addition equation. Write the sum as your next starting number.

The winner is the player whose total is closer to 100. A player who goes over 100 is out!

Roll	Open Number Line	Equation
Roll 1 ____		**1 + ____ = ____**
Roll 2 ____		
Roll 3 ____		
Roll 4 ____		
Roll 5 ____		
Roll 6 ____		

Final Score:

Types of Addition and Subtraction Word Problems

One way children attach meanings to addition and subtraction is by manipulating concrete objects and connecting their actions to symbols. They also extend their understanding of addition and subtraction by solving word problems.

Different Problem Types

Students extend their understanding of and skill with addition and subtraction by solving word problems based on different meanings or interpretations of these operations. Consider these two subtraction problems:

> *I have seven apples and Carla has four apples. How many more apples do I have than Carla?*
>
> *I had seven apples and ate four apples. How many apples are left?*

Both situations can be expressed with the same number sentence: $7 - 4 =$ _____. However, the first problem requires a *comparison* interpretation, the second, a *take away* interpretation. When an operation is reduced to symbols, it is impossible to determine which meaning is represented. In order for students to learn there are multiple interpretations of an operation, we need to give them a variety of problems to solve.

In general, difficulties with word problems do not occur because students cannot read the words but because they cannot make sense of the mathematical relationships expressed by these words. Students' understandings of the different kinds of relationships in word problems are improved by solving and discussing problems.

Join Problems and Separate Problems

Join problems and separate problems involve actions that increase or decrease a quantity, respectively. In both categories, the change occurs over time. There is an initial quantity that is changed either by adding something to it or by removing something from it, resulting in a larger or smaller final quantity.

Join (Add to)	
Result Unknown	Laina had four dolls. She bought two more. How many dolls does she have now? $4 + 2 = \square$
Change Unknown	Laina had four dolls. She bought some more dolls. Now she has six dolls. How many dolls did Laina buy? $4 + \square = 6$
Initial Quantity Unknown	Laina had some dolls. She bought two more dolls. Now she has six dolls. How many dolls did Laina have before she bought some more? $\square + 2 = 6$

Separate (Take from)	
Result Unknown	Rodney had 10 cookies. He ate three cookies. How many cookies does Rodney have left? $10 - 3 = \square$
Change Unknown	Rodney had 10 cookies. He ate some of the cookies. Now he has seven cookies left. How many cookies did Rodney eat? $10 - \square = 7$
Initial Quantity Unknown	Rodney had some cookies. He ate three cookies. Now he has seven cookies left. How many cookies did Rodney have to start with? $\square - 3 = 7$

In *join* problems and *separate* problems, the action of adding or subtracting is explicit. You can help students solve both types of problems by asking them to model these actions with objects. After solving many problems of this type, students eventually no longer need the physical model and can deal with the relationships symbolically.

The overall difficulty of a problem is partly dependent on which quantity is unknown. Join problems and separate problems in which the initial quantity or the change is unknown are more difficult than when the result is unknown. It is important to notice whether a child is able to recognize the operation that matches the situation, can represent the number sentence or equation correctly, and then can think numerically to find the answer.

It is useful for teachers to talk with students about each aspect of problem solving:

- What is the problem describing?
- How can you write that down?
- How can you find the answer?

Part-Part-Whole Problems

Part-part-whole problems do not use action verbs—action neither occurs nor is implied. Instead, relationships between a particular whole and its two separate parts are established.

Part-Part-Whole	
Whole Unknown	Five boys and three girls are on the basketball team. How many children are on the basketball team? $5 + 3 = \square$
One Part Unknown	Eight children are on the basketball team. Five are boys and the rest are girls. How many girls are on the basketball team? $5 + \square = 8$

Part-part-whole problems involve a comparison of *parts* (subsets) with the *whole* (set). The language in the problems does not suggest any action.

Compare Problems

Compare problems involve a comparison of two distinct, unconnected sets. Like part-part-whole problems, compare problems do not involve action. A relationship of difference, more than, or less than is found in compare problems.

	Part-Part-Whole
Difference Unknown	Ahmed has two brothers. Christine has three brothers. Christine has how many more brothers than Ahmed? $3 - 2 = \square$ or $2 + \square = 3$
Larger Quantity Unknown	Ahmed has two brothers. Christine has one more brother than Ahmed. How many brothers does Christine have? $2 + 1 = \square$
Smaller Quantity Unknown	Christine has one more brother than Ahmed. Christine has three brothers. How many brothers does Ahmed have? $\square + 1 = 3$ or $3 - \square = 1$

Compare and part-part-whole problems exemplify that the operations of addition and subtraction are based on the relationships between two sets or between a set and its subsets. One reason to ask students to solve a variety of problem types is so that they will generalize the meaning of these operations beyond "actions" to relationships between sets.

Students' ability to translate the words in a problem to an operation that represent the relationships presented by the words takes time and many experiences. Teachers need to present all problem types throughout the school year so that students have the opportunity to develop meaning and fluency for word problems.

Addition and Subtraction Situations

Students develop meanings for addition and subtraction as they encounter problem situations in Kindergarten, and they extend these meanings as they encounter increasingly difficult problem situations in Grade 1.

Common Situations by Grade Level

	Result Unknown	Change Unknown	Start Unknown
Add To	*A* bunnies sat on the grass. *B* more bunnies hopped there. How many bunnies are on the grass now? $A + B = \square$	*A* bunnies were sitting on the grass. Some more bunnies hopped there. Then there were *C* bunnies. How many bunnies hopped over to the first *A* bunnies? $A + \square = C$	Some bunnies were sitting on the grass. *B* more bunnies hopped there. Then there were *C* bunnies. How many bunnies were on the grass before? $\square + B = C$
Take From	*C* apples were on the table. I ate *B* apples. How many apples are on the table now? $C - B = \square$	*C* apples were on the table. I ate some apples. Then there were *A* apples. How many apples did I eat? $C - \square = A$	Some apples were on the table. I ate *B* apples. Then there were *A* apples. How many apples were on the table before? $\square - B = A$

	Total Unknown	Both Addends Unknown	Addend Unknown
Put Together/ Take Apart	*A* red apples and *B* green apples are on the table. How many apples are on the table? $A + B = \square$	Grandma has *C* flowers. How many can she put in her red vase and how many in her blue vase? $C = \square + \square$	*C* apples are on the table. *A* are red and the rest are green. How many apples are green? $A + \square = C$ $C - A = \square$

	Result Unknown	Change Unknown	Start Unknown
Compare	"How many more?" version Lucy has *A* apples. Julie has *C* apples. How many more apples does Julie have than Lucy?	"More" version suggests operation. Julie has *B* more apples than Lucy. Lucy has *A* apples. How many apples does Julie have?	"Fewer" version suggests operation. Lucy has *B* fewer apples than Julie. Julie has *C* apples. How many apples does Lucy have?
	"How many fewer?" version Lucy has *A* apples. Julie has *C* apples. How many fewer apples does Lucy have than Julie? $A + \square = C$ $C - A = \square$	"Fewer" version suggests wrong operation. Lucy has *B* fewer apples than Julie. Lucy has *A* apples. How many apples does Julie have? $A + B = \square$	"More" version suggests wrong operation. Julie has *B* more apples than Lucy. Julie has *C* apples. How many apples does Lucy have? $C - B = \square$ $\square + B = C$

Darkest shading indicates the four Kindergarten problem subtypes. Grades 1 and 2 students work with all subtypes and variants. Lighter shading indicates the four difficult subtypes or variants that students should work with in Grade 1 but need not master until Grade 2.

Classifying Addition and Subtraction Word Problems

Classify each of the following problems as join, separate, part-part-whole, or compare problems. Indicate which quantity is unknown and write a number sentence that represents the relationships expressed in each problem.

Examples

Join	Separate	Part-Part-Whole	Compare
Result Unknown Change Unknown Initial Quantity Unknown	Result Unknown Change Unknown Initial Quantity Unknown	Whole Unknown One Part Unknown	Difference Unknown Larger Quantity Unknown Smaller Quantity Unknown

1. Carlton had three model cars. His father gave him four more. How many model cars does Carlton have now?

2. Juan has nine marbles. Mary has six marbles. How many more marbles does Juan have than Mary?

3. Janice has three stickers on her lunch box and four stickers on her book bag. How many stickers does she have in all?

4. Catherine had a bag of four gummy bears. Mike gave her some more. Now Catherine has seven gummy bears. How many gummy bears did Mike give her?

5. A third grader has seven textbooks. Four textbooks are in his desk. The rest of his textbooks are in his backpack. How many textbooks are in his backpack?

6. Vladimir had some baseball cards. Chris gave him 12 more. Now Vladimir has 49 baseball cards. How many baseball cards did Vladimir have before he received some from Chris?

7. Keisha had some crayons. She gave two crayons to Tanya. Now Keisha has nine crayons. How many crayons did Keisha have in the beginning?

____

8. Anthony had nine library books on his bookshelf. He returned six books to the library. How many library books are left on his bookshelf?

____

9. There are nine board games in Joyce's room. Mariah has six fewer board games than Joyce. How many board games does Mariah have?

____

10. Eric weighed 200 pounds. During the summer, he lost some weight. Now he weighs 180 pounds. How many pounds did Eric lose?

____

11. Eli had some money. He gave his brother Johannes $5.50. Now Eli has $18.50 left. How much money did Eli have to begin with?

____

12. Graziella has four CDs. Fadia has eight more CDs than Graziella. How many CDs does Fadia have?

____

QuietWrite

Analyzing the Word Problems We Wrote

1. ***What do you notice about the types of problems we wrote?***

____

____

2. ***What are the instructional implications for what you see on the charts?***

____

____

3. ***What kinds of problems are the most challenging for your students? Why?***

____

____

Addition and Subtraction Strategies

The Common Core State Standards expect students to add and subtract using the standard algorithm by the end of Grade 4. In the early grades, students use concrete materials and drawings and develop strategies based on understanding.

You Try It.

Mentally solve the problem below and record your strategy.

28 + 29

Miguel's Strategy: Making Landmark or Friendly Numbers

Miguel: I knew 25 plus 25 was 50, but I knew each number was more than just 25. The 28 had three more, and the 29 had four more.

Teacher: So you knew 28 was the same as 25 plus three and 29 was the same as 25 plus four?

Miguel: Yes. The 25 plus 25 gave me 50, and the extra three and four gave me seven more. So I had 57 in all.

Scribing Miguel's Strategy

Lori's Strategy: Making Landmark or Friendly Numbers

Lori: I bumped both of the numbers up to friendly tens.

Teacher: What tens did you bump them to?

Lori: I made both of them a 30, so 30 plus 30 is 60. But I knew I had too much, so I minused three and got 57.

Teacher: How did you know to subtract three?

Lori: Because I added on two to the 28 and one to the 29 and that was three too much.

Scribing Lori's Strategy

Darius's Strategy: Compensation

Darius: I wanted to make an easy 10, so I took one from the 28 and gave it to the 29. That gave me 27 plus 30.

Teacher: How did you add 27 plus 30?

Darius: I started at 27 and made three jumps of 10.

Teacher: Why three jumps of 10?

Darius: Because 30 is the same as three tens. So I counted from 27 and went 37, 47, 57.

Scribing Darius's Strategy

Peggy's Strategy: Breaking Each Number Into Its Place Value

Peggy: It was easier for me to break the numbers apart and put all of the tens together and then all of the ones.

Teacher: So how did you add it up?

Peggy: I added the 20 plus 20 and got 40 and eight plus nine and got 17. I knew I had to put the 40 and 17 together next.

Teacher: How did you combine those?

Peggy: Well, 17 is the same as 10 plus seven, so I added that 10 to the 40 and got 50. Fifty plus seven is 57.

Scribing Peggy's Strategy

Strategies as Recorded by the Teacher

Miguel **28 + 29**	**Lori** **28 + 29**
(25 + 3) + (25 + 4) (25 + 25) + (3 + 4) 3 + 4 = 7 50 + 7 = 57	30 + 30 = 60 28 + 29 +2 +1 30 + 30 = 60 60 − 3 = 57
Darius **28 + 29**	**Peggy** **28 + 29**
28 + 29 −1 +1 27 + 30 +10 +10 +10 27 37 47 57	(20 + 8) + (20 + 9) (20 + 20) + (8 + 9) 40 + 17 40 + (10 + 7) (40 + 10) + 7 50 + 7 = 57

You Try It.

Record a solution to the problem below.
31 – 14

Scott's Strategy: Counting Back

Scott: I counted back. I started with 31 and counted back 14 and landed on 17.

Teacher: How did you count back?

Scott: I counted back one at a time.

Teacher: How did you know when to stop counting back?

Scott: I had to use my fingers to see when I had used 14 up.

Scribing Scott's Strategy

Ann's Strategy: Removal

Ann: I figured it out by taking chunks out.

Teacher: How did you remove the 14 in chunks?

Ann: I broke the 14 into a 10 and a one and a three. Then I took 10 from the 31 and got 21. I still needed to take away four more so I broke the four into a one and a three.

Teacher: Why did you choose to break the four into a one plus three instead of a two plus two?

Ann: Because I could take one from 21 easily to get to 20 and then take off three more.

Scribing Ann's Strategy

Strategies as Recorded by the Teacher

Scott	Ann
17 18 19 20 21 22 23 24 25 26 27 28 29 30 31	−3 −1 −10 17 20 21 31

Reflection

Day 2

What do you anticipate will be different in your classroom as a result of the new standards?

___

___

___

What are you excited about?

___

___

___

Learning From Student Work

The examples below are from a class of Kindergarten students. Students were asked to determine how many hands six people have.

Renee's Work

What I See	What I Infer From What I See	Questions About What I Infer

Madison's Work

What I See	What I Infer From What I See	Questions About What I Infer

Duncan's Work

What I See	What I Infer From What I See	Questions About What I Infer

Morgan's Work

What I See	What I Infer From What I See	Questions About What I Infer

Lizzy's Work

What I See	What I Infer From What I See	Questions About What I Infer

Gerald's Work

What I See	What I Infer From What I See	Questions About What I Infer

Student Work Background

Observing students while they work provides valuable information.

Madison's Work

Madison draws a pair of hands and then makes a line to the right "that's one person and two hands" she announces. She draws a second set of hands and says, "That's another person and two more hands. Now I have two people." She continues verbalizing her thinking and recounting the pairs as she draws each set of hands. Once she has six sets of hands, she counts the hands and records the 12.

Duncan's Work

Duncan also draws six people, and, like Madison, he recounts his figures after he completes each one. He then begins to count each hand and loses his place. He turns to Jackie, who is sitting next to him and says, "Uh-oh, I think I already counted that one. I better write this down." Jackie replies in a supportive manner: "That's okay. I do that too."

After recording the number of each hand, Duncan also writes the answer (12) at the top of his sheet. Duncan's teacher notes that he has reversed his 3, 7, and 9, but is pleased his other numbers are written correctly.

Morgan's Work

Morgan is involved with representing the story. He varies the way his characters look and includes the watermelon in his drawing. He even tries to record the names of the characters: Humpty Dumpty, Old Mother Hubbard, Jack, Jill, and Wee Willy Winky. The fact that there are six people is compelling to him, but he does not note the two-to-one relationship between people and hands. Morgan certainly knows that people have two hands, but the notion of a two-to-one correspondence that can be applied generally is an undeveloped idea. Morgan shows his recording to his teacher and they have the following conversation.

Morgan: Here's mine.

Teacher: I see you drew the characters and wrote their names as well.

Morgan: Yep, all six are here.

Teacher: Is that what these sixes mean? [*She points to the numerals on his drawing*.]

Morgan: This six is for the number of people and this six if for the number of hands.

Teacher: Can I write that? [*Morgan nods and the teacher labels the two numbers so that it is clear what they represent. She has found that when she keeps student work, she sometimes forgets its meaning. She has learned to make notes in order to jog her memory.*]

Teacher: Tell me, could there be only six hands for six people?

Morgan: No, that would be silly. [*He giggles.*]

Teacher: How many would there be?

Morgan: More.

Teacher: Do you know how many more?

Morgan: More than six.

Lizzy's Work

Lizzy counts aloud by twos, placing down a finger each time she says a number. When she has six fingers placed down, she says, "That's it, 12," and records 12 on her paper. Then she draws pairs of hands, and records the numbers she said when she counted by twos. She looks at her drawing a bit and then decides to count the number of hands in one column. Upon noting the six, she then records $6 + 6 =$ to the left of her answer so that an equation is formed.

Gerald's Work

Gerald illustrates the situation, but only partially. He then records the equation $2 + 2 = 4$. To the right of this equation, he records $4 + 4 = 8$. He then writes two more equations, adding two to eight and then two to ten. He brings his paper to his teacher and announces that the answer is 12. When the question, "How do you know?" is asked, he responds, "I found two people, doubled that, and then added the last two on."

Place-Value Assessment

The questions below explore the strategies that students use for solving numerical problems, what they understand about tens and ones, and how they relate the standard symbolism of numerals to their understanding.

Using Groups of Ten

Give the students cups with 24 color tiles each and direct them to put the tiles into groups of 10. Ask the following sequence of questions:

- How many groups of 20 and how many extras are there?
- How many tiles are there in all?
- Write the numeral that tells how many tiles there are.

Solving a Subtraction Problem

- Suppose I didn't want 24 tiles, but only 16. Can you take some away so that only 16 are left?
- Will you write the number 16?

The Meaning of the Digits

- Point to the 6 and ask, "Can you show with the tiles what the 6 means?"
- Point to the 1 and ask, "Can you show with the tiles what the 1 means?"

If the students say that the 1 means one tile, probe further with the following question:

- If these six tiles stand for the 6 and this one tile is the 1, then where do the rest of the tiles belong?

Solving an Addition Problem

- If you add 5 more tiles onto the 16, how many will you have?
- If you put 21 tiles into groups of 10, how many groups would you have? Would there be any extras?

Implementing Effective Routines

Routines give students ongoing experiences that help them practice math concepts, skills, and processes so that they may deepen their understanding of mathematics.

Quick Surveys

Survey questions can be interesting and motivating ways to engage children. Interpreting data on a graph provides students with valuable practice in counting, addition, subtraction, and using the concepts of greater than, less than, and equal to.

Key Questions

1. What do you notice about the data?
2. Which group has the most? The least?
3. How many more students like ________?

Materials
• See specific variations below

Lesson Notes

1. Decide on a question to pose to students and consider how the data will be gathered. Early in the year, use questions that have exactly two possible responses.
    - Do you like inside recess or outside recess?
    - Do you have a pet?
    - Are you wearing shoelaces?
2. Record students' responses (or have them mark their own) on the board or a piece of chart paper.

Shoelaces	No Shoelaces
X X X X X X X X X	X X X X X X X X

Shoelaces	No Shoelaces
X X X X X X X X X	X X X X X X X X
9	8

3. As the year progresses you may include questions with more than two responses, but try to choose questions with a predictable list of just a few responses.
    - In which season were you born?
    - How do you get to school?
4. Use questions such as the Key Questions to encourage students to describe, compare, and interpret the data.

Variations

Two brown bags—*Yes* and *No* Students put a cube into one of the bags to answer the question.	• Determine total number of students. • Count the number of cubes in one bag. • Students determine the number of cubes in the other bag (missing addend).
Notes:	

Jar with three different colors of cubes (each representing a different response to data question).	• Snap cubes into three separate trains. • Compare each train to a benchmark train of 10. • Emphasis is on groups of 10 and extras.
Notes:	

Yes/No Chart—Responses recorded with tally marks.	• Count tally marks by fives and by tens. • Make comparison statements.
Notes:	

Binder—Use clothespins to respond to the Yes side or the No side.	• Clothespins are clipped to large ten-frames. • Make explicit connections between the numeric symbol and the clothespins that are organized into groups of tens and leftovers. (17 is one full 10 and 7 more.)
Notes:	

Breaking Numbers Apart

This routine gives students an opportunity to create equivalent expressions and explore number composition and part-whole relationships. In addition, it helps students use operations flexibly and recognize relationships between operations.

Key Questions

In what ways can you break apart the number ________?

How do you know that this is a true equation?

Materials
• snap cubes (for K–1)

Lesson Notes (K–1)

- Record the number of the day on chart paper or the board and distribute snap cubes.
- Direct students to think of different ways to break apart the number of the day. Say something like, "I want you to break apart your train in one place so that you have two trains."
- Ask students to describe their trains. Record sketches of trains and corresponding number sentences.
- When students are ready, extend this routine to include more than two addends.

Lesson Notes (Grade 2)

1. Ask students to think about how to break apart the number of the day. Allot about one minute for them to share their ideas with a partner.
2. As volunteers share with the class, record equations on the board.

   $10 + 10 + 4 = 24$

   $(10 \times 2) + 4 = 24$

   $5 + 5 + 5 + 5 + 4 = 24$

3. Periodically ask students to prove an equation is true. Also ask questions to encourage students to make connections between different equations.
4. As students gain experience, this activity can be extended by introducing constraints: use only coin values, use only addition, use more than one operation, use at least three numbers, cannot use zero.

Reflect On	Ideas to Maximize Instruction
Common Core Connections	
Probing Questions	
Grade-Level Modifications	
Helpful Tips	
Additional	

Estimating

Estimating is an important skill that helps students develop their number sense. Using concrete objects to estimate and count helps children visualize the quantities that numbers represent.

Key Questions (K–1)

Materials

- plastic bag (for K–1) or glass jar (Grade 2)
- 20–40 snap cubes

- About how many cubes do you think ______ can hold in his hand?
- This is what a handful of cubes looks like. Now how many cubes do you think ______ can hold in his hand?
- What can help you make a good estimate?
- Do you think ______ (second student) can pick up more or fewer cubes than ______?
- How many more cubes did ______ pick up than ______?

Lesson Notes (K–1)

1. Show students a small amount of cubes and ask them how many there are.
2. Ask one student to take a handful of cubes from the plastic bag filled with cubes.
3. Ask the class to estimate how many cubes there are in the handful. Record estimates on the board, and then count the cubes to determine the total. Return the cubes to the bag.
4. Ask a second student to take a handful of cubes from the bag. Ask the students to predict whether the second handful will be larger than or smaller than the first handful. Count the cubes and compare the totals. Return the cubes to the bag.
5. Finally, take a handful. Lay the cubes in trains of five. Ask the students to count the cubes. If necessary, help them count—both by fives and by ones.

Key Questions (Grade 2)

- About how many cubes do you think are in the jar?
- What if we count by twos (or fives or tens)? Will there still be xx cubes? Explain.
- This is what 10 cubes looks like. How many cubes do you think there are inside the jar?
- If I took the cubes out of the jar and snapped them together in trains of 10 cubes each, how many trains of 10 would I have? How many extras would there be? Explain.
- What if there were 45 cubes in the jar? How many trains of 10? How many extra? Explain.

Lesson Notes (Grade 2)

1. Show the students a jar filled with cubes.
2. Students estimate the number of cubes. Record the estimates on the board.
3. Remove 10 cubes from the jar and ask students if they want to change their estimates.
4. Count cubes in the jar by ones, then twos, and then fives, asking students whether the number of cubes will stay the same or change each time.
5. Ask students to predict how many trains of 10 we will have. Ask volunteers to share their thinking. Then, snap the cubes together in trains of 10 to confirm students' thinking.

Reflect On	Ideas to Maximize Instruction
Common Core Connections	
Probing Questions	
Grade-Level Modifications	
Helpful Tips	
Additional	

Grow and Shrink

***Grow and Shrink* helps students learn about number relationships, provides counting practice, and serves as an informal context for exploring addition and subtraction.**

Key Questions

1. How many dots is ______ and ______ more? How do you know?
2. How many cubes should you put on your ten-frame? Explain.
3. How many cubes do we need to make 10?

Materials
• ten-frame, 1 per student • cubes or counters, 10 per student • 2 dice (0–5)

Lesson Notes

1. Roll the two dice. Record the roll on the board using two boxes to represent the dice and dots to represent the two numbers rolled. Students should work together to determine the total.
2. Students represent the total with cubes on their ten-frames.
3. Continue rolling the dice. Record each roll on the board. After students determine the total rolled, remind them to place cubes on their ten-frames to match the sum shown on the two dice. Say something like, "Now, because there are seven dots showing on the dice, change your ten-frame so that there are seven cubes on it."
4. Ask, "Who can tell us how you figured out how to put seven cubes on your ten-frame?" Some students will clear the frame and then show the new quantity. Other students will start from the current number and add or subtract as needed.
5. To extend the activity, use two ten-frames and up to four of the 0–5 dice.

Reflect On	Ideas to Maximize Instruction
Common Core Connections	
Probing Questions	
Grade-Level Modifications	
Helpful Tips	
Additional	

Double Ten-Frame

Note: Enlarge to create a demonstration version of the double ten-frame.

Measuring Area

Students use square tiles to estimate and then measure the area of different shapes. Using colors to group sets of 10 provides the opportunity to make connections between the concrete tiles and the abstract numerical symbol.

Key Questions

1. Here are 10 tiles. How many tiles do you think will cover all of your shape?
2. If a shape is covered with 24 tiles, how many colors will there be? Explain.

Materials

- color tiles, about 40 per pair of students
- copies of outlines of varying shapes and sizes

Lesson Notes

1. Place 10 color tiles of one color inside one of the shape outlines.

2. Together with the students, count the 10 tiles, touching each tile as you count.
3. Ask students to estimate how many tiles will fill the area of the shape, based on what they have discovered so far.
4. Place 10 more tiles of a different color in the area of the shape. Ask students to make a new estimate of how many tiles will fill the shape.
5. Continue adding groups of 10 tiles until the shape is completely filled. Count the tiles with the students, first by ones and then by tens.

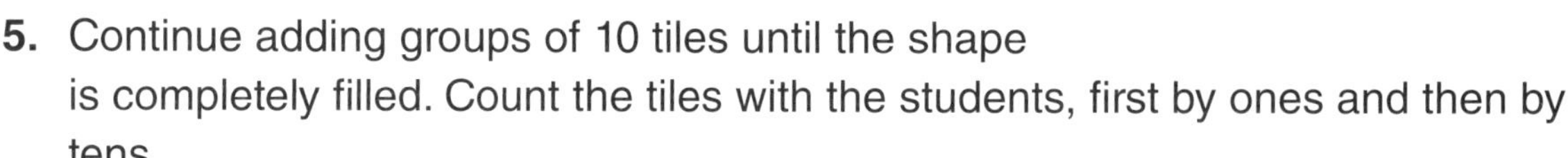

6. Record the total number. Make connections between the written numeral and the tiles. For example, for 24 there will be two groups of 10 and four extra tiles.

Reflect On	Ideas to Maximize Instruction
Common Core Connections	
Probing Questions	
Grade-Level Modifications	
Helpful Tips	
Additional	

Balancing Number Puzzles

In Grades 3–5, extend students' understanding about place value with whole numbers into place value with decimals.

Lesson Notes

Materials
• base ten blocks (optional)
• paper, 1 sheet per student

In this lesson, students use their knowledge of place value to solve balancing number puzzles. They strengthen their number sense as they apply their computation skills in addition and subtraction to find missing addends. The idea of balance is represented using drawings that show both sides in balance, thus indicating the sides are equivalent.

Introduction

1. Draw the following on the board:

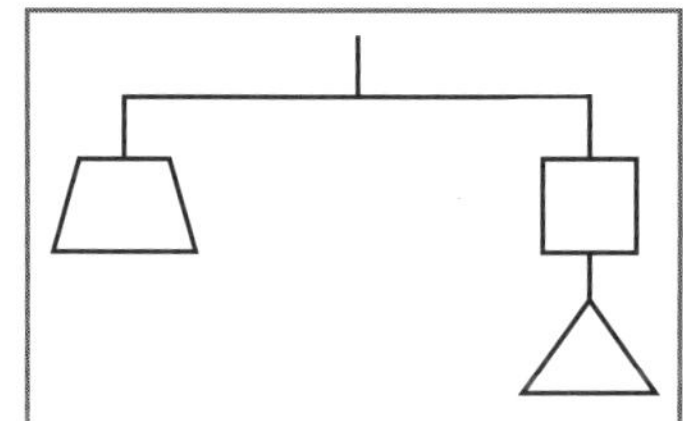

2. Ask students, "What does this remind you of?" As they share ideas, guide them as needed to make connections between the drawing and things in their world that balance.
3. Write 64 and 100 as shown.

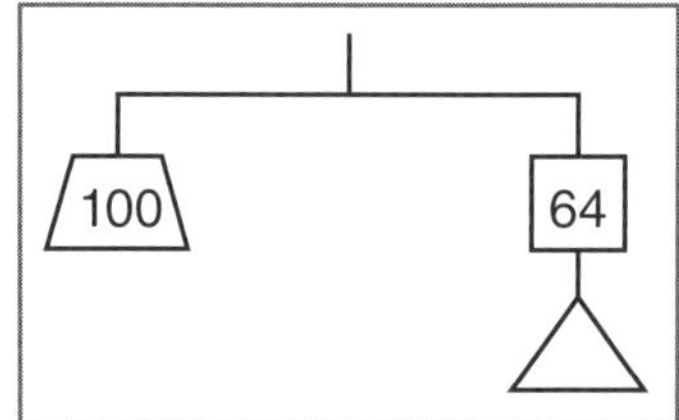

Ask students, "Now that I've added some numbers to my picture, what do you know?" Have students share their ideas with their partners and then with the whole group.

Divide the empty shape into two halves and label the left half *Tens* and the right half *Ones*. Ask students, "How many more tens do I need to add to 64 to get to 100?" Share and discuss students' ideas.

4. Using base ten blocks, check the needed number of tens. Using a document camera, project a flat. To show 64, lay on top of the flat six tens and four ones. Together determine the number of tens and ones needed to completely cover the flat. Complete the puzzle. Lead a discussion about why the solution makes sense.

5. Introduce the second problem by drawing the following:

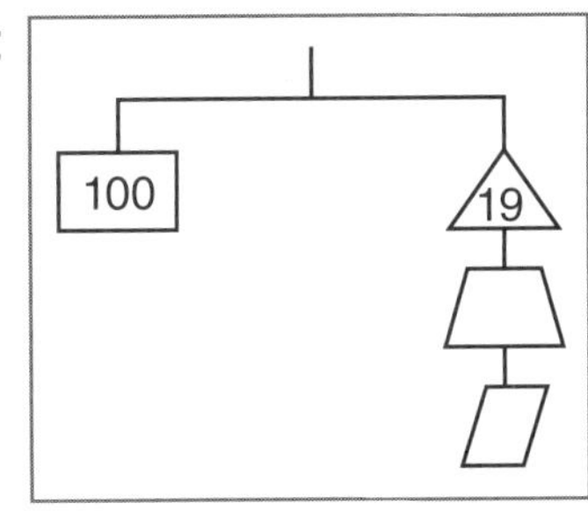

Ask students, "How is this puzzle different from the first one?"

Because there are two open shapes, there is more than one correct solution to the puzzle. Encourage several students to share.

6. The following puzzle provides an extension from place value with whole numbers to place value with decimals. It is important to prompt students' thinking about equality before asking for solutions. Students should communicate that the total of the right side must be 1.0 and that the value of the triangle and parallelogram together must be the same as the value of the trapezoid.

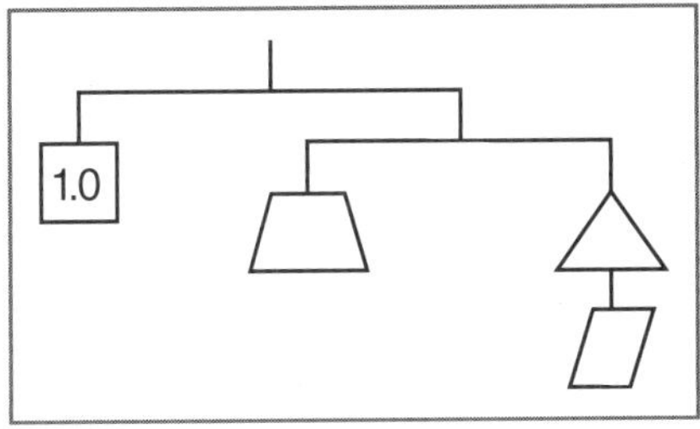

7. The following are more ideas for puzzles with decimals.

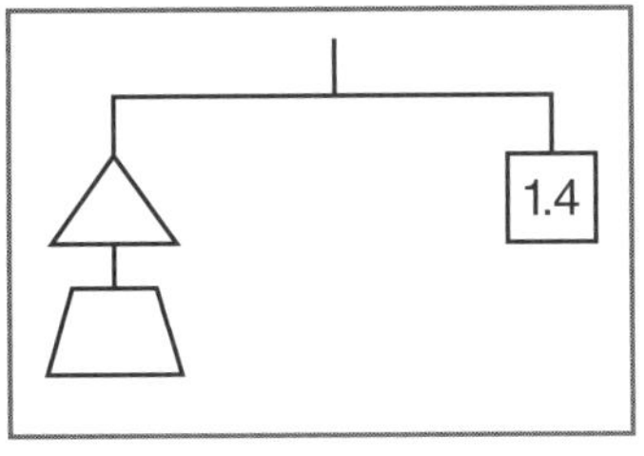

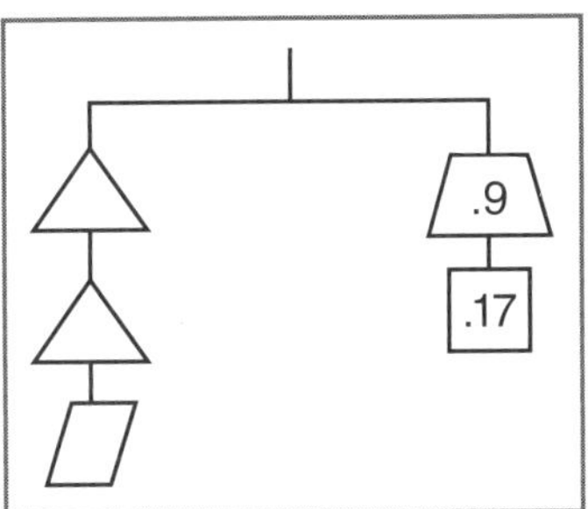

Exploration

8. After numerous examples, and likely on another day of instruction, model for students how to create a balancing numbers puzzle. Draw the following on the board:

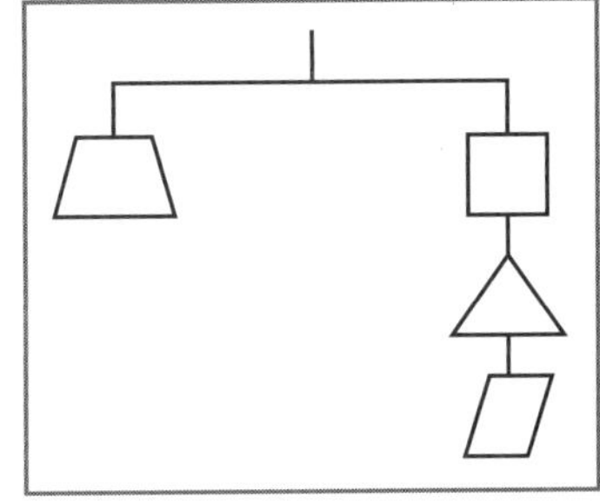

Involve students in thinking about where to add numbers. Ask, "Where would it make sense to start?" Discuss different ideas from students.

9. Instruct students to create their own balancing numbers puzzles. They should draw the puzzle on one side of the paper and solve it in two or three ways. Then, on the other side, draw the puzzle for someone else to solve.

   A benefit of having students draw their own puzzles is it allows different children to grapple with the same idea at their own levels of understanding.

10. As students work, circulate through the class, observing and answering questions as needed.

Summarization

11. Ask volunteers to share their puzzles. Other students share possible solutions to the puzzles. Use questions such as the following to facilitate a discussion.
    - Who would like to share what you are thinking?
    - Is there another way to fill in the shapes?
    - How can you justify that your solution works?

Reflection: Considering the Role of Place Value

1. How have the experiences and discussion affected your thinking about the role of place value in developing understanding about operations?

____

____

____

Sketch a balanced number puzzle that would be helpful for your students to discuss.

Investigating Rectangles

Provide as many opportunities as possible for students to see how different mathematical topics relate to one another. This lesson helps build a connection between the numerical concept of multiplication and the geometric concept of area.

Introduction

Materials
• 50 color tiles per group of 4 students • 1 sheet of $\frac{1}{2}$-inch grid paper per student

1. Begin the investigation by asking students to work with a partner and use 12 color tiles to build a rectangle that is completely filled in with no holes.
2. Ask students to describe the rectangles they built. Sketch the rectangles on the board or chart paper. Discuss and label the dimensions of each rectangle. Clarify that rectangles that have the same dimensions, regardless of orientation, are considered the same rectangle, and only one example is needed. Examples of a 3-by-4, 2-by-6, and 1-by-12 should be shared.
3. Ask partners to investigate two more numbers, 16 and 7, to allow an opportunity for clarifying questions and to strengthen students' understanding of the investigation. Using the number 16 introduces the idea that a square is a special type of rectangle. Because 7 is a prime number, students will discover that some numbers only have one possible rectangle.

Exploration

4. Share the parameters for the whole investigation. Small groups work together and use color tiles to find all the possible arrays for the numbers 1–25. Then, they cut out the arrays from the $\frac{1}{2}$-inch grid paper. Encourage students to first discuss how their groups will organize and share the work.
5. As groups work, circulate and give suggestions and reminders as needed. Ask questions such as:
   - How are you keeping track of which ones you have finished?
   - Can you find a way to check with each other to make sure you have found all the rectangles for each number?

Summarization

6. Create a posting area. Number from 1 to 25. Consider asking a group that finishes early to tape their rectangles under the corresponding numbers. Other groups can contribute if they identify missing rectangles.
7. Use the questions below to facilitate a discussion. Focus students on patterns and introduce vocabulary when appropriate. Possible vocabulary words include: multiples, square numbers, prime numbers, factors, and products.

Discussion Questions

1. For which numbers are there rectangles that have sides with two squares on them? Write the numbers from smallest to largest.
2. For which numbers are there rectangles that have sides with three squares on them? Write the numbers from smallest to largest.
3. For which numbers are there rectangles that have sides with four squares on a side? Write the numbers from smallest to largest.
4. For which numbers are there rectangles that have sides with five squares on a side? Write the numbers from smallest to largest.
5. Which numbers have rectangles that are squares?
6. How many squares are in the next larger square you can make?

7. What is the smallest number with exactly two different rectangles? Three different rectangles? Four?

8. Which numbers have only one rectangle? List them from smallest to largest.

Reflection: Promoting Productive Mathematical Discussions

1. What is the role of the focused questions used to structure the discussion about different rectangles?

2. What did you notice about how mathematical vocabulary was introduced?

Building the Multiplication Chart

In this activity, students use their arrays as a manipulative that supports their understanding of the numbers in the multiplication table.

Introduction

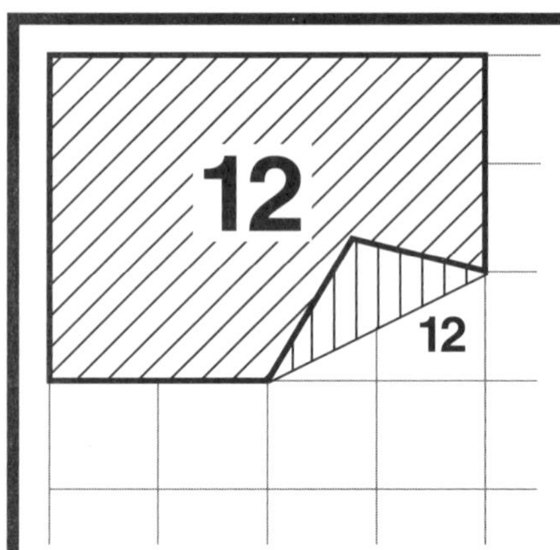

1. Demonstrate using a whole sheet of $\frac{1}{2}$-inch grid paper and the 3-by-4 rectangle that was cut in the previous activity.
2. Align the corner of the rectangle in the upper left corner of the grid paper. Lift the lower right corner of the rectangle, and in the square under that corner write the number 12.
3. Remove the rectangle and say something like, "Now I will use the same rectangle, but in the other position." Then, rotate the same rectangle 90° and align top, left corner in the same place of the grid paper. Again, lift the lower right corner, and write 12 underneath.
4. Repeat this process for the 2-by-6 and the 1-by-12 rectangles, writing 12 in four additional squares. Then, demonstrate the process again using the two rectangles for the number 9

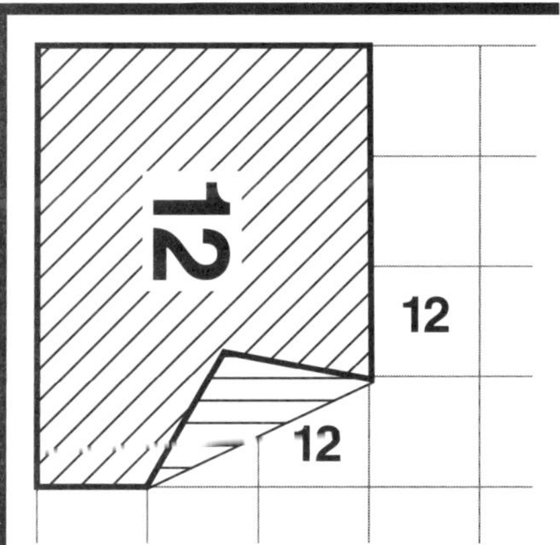

Exploration

5. Direct students to follow this process for each of the rectangles that will fit on the grid paper.
6. Circulate to observe students. Ask questions to encourage students to notice patterns.
   - What number do you think might come before that space? After?
   - What is different about the squares? (4, 16, 25)

Summarization

7. Discuss the patterns on the chart. Focus students' attention on the patterns that are familiar to them: the 2s, 5s, and 10s. Model how to continue those rows as far as the sheet allows. Repeat this for the 2, 5, and 10 columns.
8. Encourage students to extend other multiples.
9. After students have completed their multiplication tables to at least a 12-by-12 array, ask them to look for patterns. Possible patterns include:
   - Everything in the 11s column is double-digit
   - On our multiplication table, for $10 \times n$ just add a zero to that number (n) and you have the answer
   - If you multiply the number at the top of the column by the number at the left of a row, the product will be where the row and column intersect
   - On the even-numbered rows or columns, all of the products are an even number; on the odd-numbered columns and rows, the products are odd, even, odd, even, odd, even
   - For the 9s, the product will add up to nine
   - In the 6th column or row, if you add the digits in the product, you get the pattern 6, 3, 9, 6, 3, 9 . . .

Reflection: Fostering Understanding

1. How do these experiences with multiplication compare to lessons typically found in textbooks?

____

____

____

____

2. What will you need in order to feel confident facilitating this type of investigation?

____

____

____

____

$\frac{1}{2}$-inch Grid Paper

1-inch Grid Paper

Silent Multiplication

Exploring patterns in factors and products helps students develop understanding of the mathematics underlying multidigit multiplication.

Lesson Notes

Note: Prior to the lesson, plan the problem strings to introduce to students.

1. Explain to students the rules for a silent lesson:
   - A star drawn on the board indicates the beginning of the activity and silence by everyone, including the teacher.
   - When a problem is written on the board, students should indicate when they know the answer by putting their thumbs-up.
   - When an answer is written, students should indicate agreement with thumbs-up, disagreement with thumbs-down, or indecision or confusion with thumbs-sideways.
2. Draw a star on the board to indicate that it's time for silence. For an introductory experience, write a multiplication problem on the board that all students can solve, for example 1×2.
3. Wait for students to show thumbs-up.
4. Hand the chalk or marker to a student and indicate that he or she should write the product on the board. Wait for the other students to indicate agreement, disagreement, or indecision or confusion by putting their thumbs-up, down, or sideways.
5. Write a second related problem (for example, 2×2) under the first problem. When students are ready, hand the chalk to a volunteer to write the answer. Other students should use their thumbs to indicate agreement, disagreement, or indecision or confusion. Erase the star, indicating talking is permitted.
6. Lead a discussion about how the two problems are related and how students can use what they know from the first problem to help them solve the second problem.
7. While steps 1 through 6 model for students the basic structure of this activity, emphasize to the students the need to be silent and think about how to apply what they already know to solve each new problem. Draw a star and continue with the silent lesson for a series of four or more related problems.

8. Erase the star and lead a class discussion about how students used what they knew about one problem to solve another. Pose such questions as the following:
    - How are these two problems related?
    - What is the same about these problems?
    - What is different?
    - What happened to the factors?
    - What happened to the products?
9. In future lessons, explore new ideas such as multiplying by 10. Leave time at the end of class for students to respond to the following prompt, "Something I learned playing Silent Multiplication is . . ."
10. Continue on other days with other sequences of problems.

Doubling One Factor

$3 \times 4 =$

$4 \times 6 =$

$4 \times 12 =$

$4 \times 24 =$

$8 \times 24 =$

$24 \times 16 =$

$32 \times 24 =$

Multiplying by 10

$4 \times 1 =$

$4 \times 10 =$

$40 \times 10 =$

$41 \times 10 =$

$45 \times 10 =$

$451 \times 10 =$

Multiplying by 10 and multiples of 10

$1 \times 12 =$

$10 \times 12 =$

$10 \times 24 =$

$20 \times 24 =$

$40 \times 24 =$

Factor Fiddling

Factor Fiddling is an independent activity that extends students' understanding of multiplication. After students have time to investigate, it is important to lead a whole-class discussion to have them present what they learned.

Introduction

1. Write 5×3 on the board. Ask students what new problems can be made by doubling only one of the factors. As students share, record both possibilities: 5×6 and 10×3.
2. Direct students to solve all three problems and compare the products. How would they describe the relationships?
3. Repeat with another problem and ask students to pose conjectures about what they notice.

Exploration

4. Investigate what happens to the product of two factors when you fiddle with one or both of the factors in other ways:
   - Halve both factors.
   - Double both factors.
   - Double one factor and halve the other one.

Summarization

5. Before initiating a classroom discussion, remind students of the three questions they investigated. Ask them to talk with a partner about their findings.
6. Invite volunteers to share. Consider asking multiple students to post examples on the board so that there are common examples to discuss. As students share generalizations, push them to justify why that is true.
7. Many students will benefit from a visual model. Arrays can be cut from grid paper to model examples.

Multiplication and Division

Beginning in third grade, students focus on understanding the meaning and properties of multiplication and division and on finding products of single-digit multiplying and related quotients. These skills and understandings are crucial.

Understanding Relationships

Multiplication and division have always been important topics in elementary school mathematics. However, in the past, instruction has focused primarily on helping students develop procedural competency with basic facts and paper-and-pencil algorithms. This procedural competency is an important goal, but recent research makes it clear that students also need to develop deep conceptual knowledge of multiplication and division in order to apply and use these operations to solve problems.

Conceptual knowledge is based on understanding relationships. Relationships that represent multiplication and division can be expressed using pictures, graphs, objects, symbols, and words. Since everyday mathematics is almost always applied in the context of words, not symbols, it is important for students to understand the relationship inherent in multiplication and division problems. In addition, students' understanding of these relationships helps them generalize their knowledge and apply it to related concepts in algebra.

Likewise, students must understand the language of multiplication and division situations.

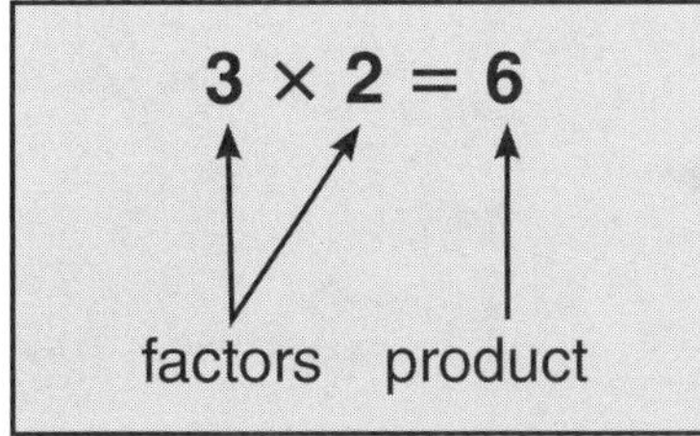

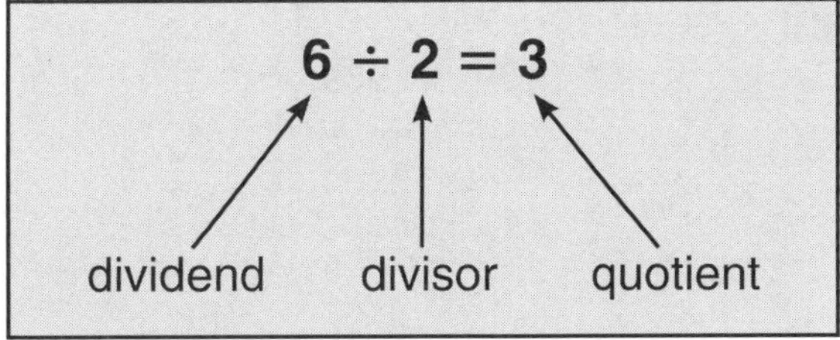

In some division expressions there is also a remainder.

factor × factor = product

dividend ÷ divisor = quotient + remainder

Middle school students who have difficulty rewriting division sentences with and without remainders as multiplication sentences may not be secure in their understanding of the inverse relationship between the two operations.

Analyzing Multiplication and Division Word Problems

One aspect of understanding multiplication and division is being able to make sense of and solve word problems. Research suggests that children in the elementary grades need experiences with a variety of problem types.

Sample Word Problems

Compare the word problems you wrote with the examples below. How are they similar? How are they different?

Asymmetrical

Equal Groups

Mark has 4 bags of apples.
There are 6 apples in each bag.
How many apples does Mark have altogether?
(Equal Groups/Product Unknown)

Mark has 24 apples.
He wants to share them equally among his 4 friends.
How many apples will each friend receive?
(Equal Groups/Size of Groups Unknown)

Mark has 24 apples.
He puts them into bags containing 6 apples each.
How many bags does Mark use?
(Equal Groups/Number of Groups Unknown)

Rate

If apples cost 40 cents each,
how much does Jill have to pay for 5 apples?
(Rate/Product Unknown)

Peter walks 12 miles in 3 hours.
How many miles per hour (how fast) does he walk?
(Rate/Partitive Division)

Marisol jogs 9 miles at a rate of 3 miles per hour.
How many hours does it take Marisol to jog the 9 miles?
(Rate/Quotitive Division)

Multiplicative Compare

Jill picks 6 apples.
Mark picks 4 times as many apples as Jill.
How many apples does Mark pick?
(Compare/Product Unknown)

This month Mark saved 5 times as much money as he did last month.
If he saved $35 this month, how much did he save last month?
(Compare/Size of Set Unknown)

Symmetrical

Rectangular Array

The perimeter of a vegetable garden measures 40 feet by 15 feet.
What is the area of the garden?
(Rectangular Array/Multiplication)

The student council made a 2,160 square-inch banner that is 36 inches wide.
How long is the banner?
(Rectangular Array/Missing Factor Division Problem)

Cartesian Product

Sam bought 4 pairs of pants and 3 jackets, and they can all be mixed and matched.
How many different outfits consisting of a pair of pants and jacket does Sam have?
(Cartesian Product [combinations]/Product Unknown)

Sam bought some new pants and jackets. He has a total of 12 different outfits.
If he bought 4 pairs of pants, how many jackets did Sam buy?
(Cartesian Product [combinations]/Missing Factor Division Problem)

Two Types of Word Problems

Asymmetrical and symmetrical are two broad types of multiplication and division problems. To help students understand the relationships in these problem types, guide them to model situations and discuss relationships between the quantities.

Asymmetrical and Symmetrical Situations

The resource *Math Matters* by Suzanne H. Chapin and Art Johnson is a valuable tool for supporting teachers in deepening their understanding of mathematics and considering important aspects of instruction. Read the following excerpt to better understand problem types.

> There are 15 cars in the parking lot and each car has 4 tires. How many tires are there in all?

In the problem above, the 4 represents the amount of one group, 15 represents the number of groups and also acts as the multiplier. These roles are not interchangeable. If you switch the numbers (4 cars with 15 tires each), you have a different problem. This is an example of an asymmetrical situation.

In symmetrical situations, on the other hand, the quantities have interchangeable roles. It is not clear which factor is the multiplier. In the problem below, either number can be the width or the length and either can be used as the multiplier.

> What is the area of a room that is 10 feet by 12 feet?

Subcategories of Asymmetrical and Symmetrical Situations

There are three subcategories of asymmetrical problems:

- Equal grouping
- Rate
- Multiplicative compare

There are two subcategories of symmetrical problems:

- Rectangular array
- Cartesian product

Each subcategory includes both multiplication and division problems, depending on which quantity is unknown. Students need to work with all types of multiplication and division problems in order to make sense of the relationships inherent to each type and to extend their understanding of these operations beyond mere procedure.

Equal-Grouping Problems: Multiplication

In equal-grouping multiplication problems, one factor tells the number of things in a group and the other factor tells the number of equal-size groups. This second factor acts as a multiplier.

> There are 4 basketball teams at the tournament and each team has 5 players. How many players are in the tournament?

In the problem above, the factor 5 indicates the number of players in one group, and the factor 4 indicates the number of equal groups of 5. The 4 acts as the multiplier. Equal-grouping problems are easy to model with pictures or by using repeated addition.

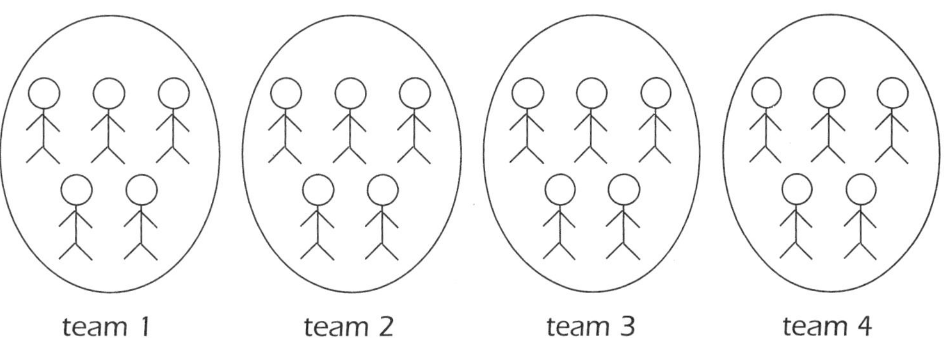

Equal-Grouping Problems: Division

In an equal-grouping division problem either the number of groups or the number of objects in each group is unknown. These two types of division situations are referred to as quotitive division and partitive division, respectively.

Partitive Division

Twenty-four apples need to be placed into 8 paper sacks. How many apples will you put in each sack if you want the same number in each sack?

The action involved is one of dividing or partitioning a set into a predetermined number of groups. When teaching division, teachers often choose partitive examples to highlight equal sharing. For example, students are instructed to divide a set number of counters into four equal groups by distributing the counters one at a time into four piles. When partitive division problems are the only examples students are exposed to, they often struggle to make sense of quotitive division problems.

Quotitive Division

These types of problems are sometimes referred to as repeated subtraction problems. The number of objects in a group is known, but the number of groups is unknown.

I have 24 apples. How many paper sacks will I be able to fill if I put 3 apples into each sack?

The action involved in quotitive division is one of subtracting out predetermined amounts. When modeling the problem, a student would likely subtract 3 objects from a group of 24 and then count the groups of 3 he or she removed.

The standard long division algorithm uses the quotitive interpretation of division. The divisor represents the number in one group, and this amount is repeatedly subtracted from the dividend. The number of multiples (or groups) of the divisor that are subtracted from the dividend is the answer. Students benefit from exposure to both types of division examples so that they internalize that two actions, subtracting and partitioning, are used to find quotients.

Rate Problems

Rate problems involve a rate: a special type of ratio in which two different quantities or things are compared. Common rates are miles per gallon, wages per hour, and points per game. Rates are frequently expressed as unit rates, that is, one of the quantities in the ratio is given as a unit (e.g., price per single pound or miles per single hour). In rate problems, one number identifies the unit rate and the other tells the number of sets and acts as the multiplier. In the problem below, the unit rate is $7 per single ticket and the multiplier is four.

> Concert tickets cost $7 each. How much will it cost for a family of 4 to attend the concert?

Rate problems can also be expressed as division situations.

> On the Hollingers' trip to New York City, they drove 400 miles and used 12 gallons of gasoline. How many miles per gallon did they average?

> Jasmine spent $108 on some new CDs. Each CD cost $18. How many did she buy?

Multiplicative Compare Problems

In these problems, one number identifies the quantity in one group or set while the other number is the comparison factor.

> Catherine read 12 books. Elizabeth read 4 times as many. How many books did Elizabeth read?

The number 12 tells us the amount in a group, and the number 4 tells us how many of these groups are needed. The relational language in multiplicative compare problems (e.g., times as many, times greater) is difficult for all students, especially so for those for whom English is a second language. Students make sense of both the language and the relationships the language implies by discussing and modeling these problems.

Rectangular Array Problems

These problems are commonly known as area problems and are often used to introduce the idea of multiplication. Students are presented with an array and asked to label the two sides of the array and determine the total number of square units in the array.

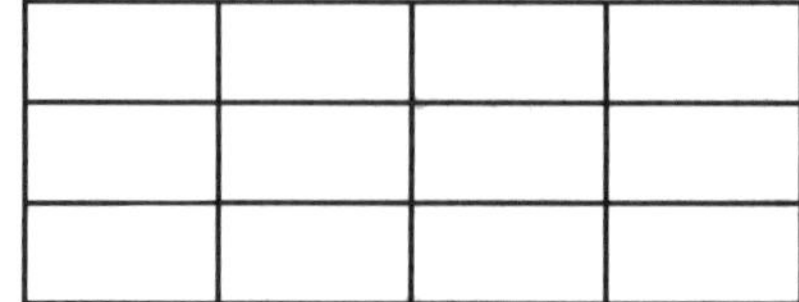

In rectangular array problems, the role of the factors is interchangeable. For instance, when finding the area of the array above, neither the 3 nor the 4 is clearly the multiplier.

Cartesian Product Problems

Cartesian product problems involve two sets and the pairing of elements between the sets. These problems entail a number of combinations.

> Pete's Deli stocks 4 types of cold cuts and 2 types of cheese. How many different sandwiches made of one type of meat and one type of cheese are possible?

In these problems, like the rectangular array problems, neither of the two factors is clearly the multiplier. Students tend to use tree diagrams to solve Cartesian product problems, in order to help them find all the combinations. For example, for the problem above, a student might use a diagram like this:

Meats	**Cheese**	**Sandwich Combinations**
turkey	swiss	turkey swiss
	cheddar	turkey cheddar
ham	swiss	ham swiss
	cheddar	ham cheddar
bologna	swiss	bologna swiss
	cheddar	bologna cheddar
roast beef	swiss	roast beef swiss
	cheddar	roast beef cheddar

Another way to solve Cartesian product problems is to construct a rectangular array like the one below. The number of columns (4) and the number of rows (2) are the factors in the problem.

	Ham	Turkey	Salami	Roast Beef
Swiss	Swiss/Ham	Swiss/Turkey	Swiss/Salami	Swiss/RB
Cheddar	Cheddar/Ham	Cheddar/Turkey	Cheddar/Salami	Cheddar/RB

This representation shows how finding the number of combinations of 4 luncheon meats and 2 cheeses is similar to finding the area of a rectangle that is 4 units by 2 units.

Missing Factor Division Problems

Both rectangular array and Cartesian product problems have related division problems called missing factor division problems.

> Sukai has 24 different outfits consisting of a blouse and a pair of pants. She has four pairs of pants. How many blouses does she own?

Although this problem can be solved by dividing 24 by 4, the relationship can also be expressed as $4 \times \square = 24$. Many students convert division problems to the inverse operation of multiplication, hence the name missing factor.

Multiplication and Division Situations

Exploring many different types of word problems contributes to developing a strong and complete conceptual knowledge of multiplication and division.

Three Major Problem Types for Grades 3–5

Students in Grades 3–5 solve equal group, array, and compare problems.

	$A \times B = \square$	$A \times \square = C$ and $C \div A = \square$	$\square \times B = C$ and $C \div B = \square$
Equal Groups of Objects	*Unknown Product* There are A bags with B plums in each bag. How many plums are there in all?	*Group Size Unknown* If C plums are shared equally into A bags, then how many plums will be in each bag?	*Number of Groups Unknown* If C plums are to be packed B to a bag, then how many bags are needed?
Arrays of Objects	*Unknown Product* There are A rows of apples with B apples in each row. How many apples are there?	*Equal groups language Unknown Factor* If C apples are arranged into A equal rows, how many apples will be in each row?	*Unknown Factor* If C apples are arranged into equal rows of B apples, how many rows will there be?
Arrays of Objects	*Unknown Product* The apples in the grocery window are in A rows and B columns. How many apples are there?	*Row and column language Unknown Factor* If C apples are arranged into an array with A rows, how many columns of apples are there?	*Unknown Factor* If C apples are arranged into an array with 8 columns, how many rows are there?

Common Core Standards Writing Team. (2013, May 29). Progressions for the Common Core State Standards in Mathematics (draft). Grades K–5, Operations and Algebraic Thinking. Tucson, AZ: Institute for Mathematics and Education, University of Arizona.

	$A \times B = \square$	$A \times \square = C$ and $C \div A = \square$	$\square \times B = C$ and $C \div B = \square$
Compare	*Larger Unknown* A blue hat costs \$B. A red hat costs A times as much as the blue hat. How much does the red hat cost?	*Smaller Unknown* $A < 1$ A red hat costs \$C, and that is A times as much as a blue hat costs. How much does a blue hat cost?	*Multiplier Unknown* A red hat costs \$C, and a blue hat costs \$B. How many times as much does the red hat cost as the blue hat?
	Smaller Unknown A blue hat costs \$B. A red hat costs A as much as the blue hat. How much does the red hat cost?	*Larger Unknown* $A > 1$ A red hat costs \$C, and that is A of the cost of a blue hat. How much does a blue hat cost?	*Multiplier Unknown* A red hat costs \$C, and a blue hat costs \$B. What fraction of the cost of the blue hat is the cost of the red hat?

Common Core Standards Writing Team. (2013, May 29). Progressions for the Common Core State Standards in Mathematics (draft). Grades K–5, Operations and Algebraic Thinking. Tucson, AZ: Institute for Mathematics and Education, University of Arizona.

Classifying Word Problems

This page is provided to give you practice identifying the different problem types.

Classification of Multiplication and Division Problems

Decide on the category in which the problem belongs. Identify whether each problem is a multiplication or a division problem.

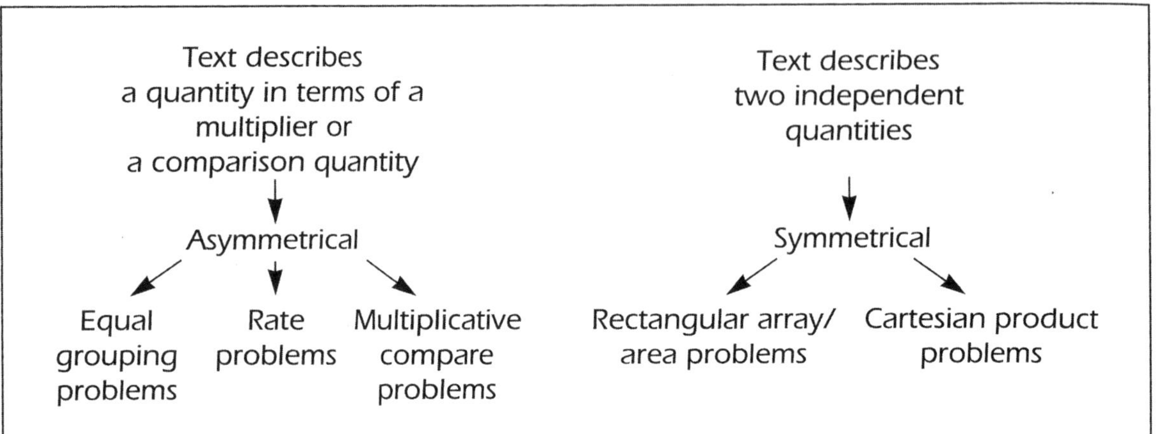

1. Five children are planning to share a bag of 53 pieces of bubble gum. How many will each get?

2. Pies cost $7.50 each. Paula bought 5 pies. How much did they cost in all?

3. Peter bicycled 36 miles in 3 hours. How fast did Peter bike?

4. A restaurant offers 5 appetizers and 7 main courses. How many different meals can be ordered if a meal consists of 1 appetizer and 1 main course?

5. This year Mark saved $420. Last year he saved $60. How many times as much money did he save this year than last year?

6. This year Maddie saved 4 times as many dollars as she saved last year. Last year she saved $18. How many dollars has she saved this year?

7. Each jar holds 8 ounces of liquid. If there are 46 ounces of water in a pitcher, how many jars are needed to hold the liquid?

8. Leroy has a 1,440-square-inch piece of fabric that is 60 inches wide. How long is the fabric?

9. Sam Slick is really excited about his new clothing purchases. He bought 4 pairs of pants and a number of jackets, and they can all be mixed and matched. Sam can wear a different outfit consisting of jacket and pants 12 days in a row. How many jackets did he buy?

10. Liana walked 12 miles at a rate of 4 miles per hour. How many hours did it take Liana to walk the 12 miles?

11. Maria earned $24. She earned 4 times as much as Jill. How much did Jill earn?

12. The foundation of the house measures 70 feet by 25 feet. What is the square footage of the ground floor of the house?

Division Computation

Many mathematics educators recommend providing opportunities for students to develop, use, and discuss a variety of methods instead of teaching students standard algorithms as the only or best ways to compute with paper and pencil.

Partial Quotients Algorithm

Record an example of this algorithm to use later as a reference.

Discussion Questions: 496 ÷ 8 =

1. How does the succession of the problems provide a scaffold for students to solve 496 ÷ 8?
2. How do students build upon their understanding of multiplication to divide?
3. What evidence demonstrates students' understanding of place value?
4. What is the purpose of the teacher repeatedly asking students to explain where their answers are in the strategy?

Reflection: Procedures With Understanding

How do you think that working with different strategies and building number sense could prevent the common errors often made with the standard division algorithm?

The Divisor Stays the Same

This lesson focuses on the relationships among dividends, divisors, quotients, and remainders expressed in whole numbers. Students investigate the patterns that occur in quotients when the divisor stays the same.

Investigating Patterns

Investigate patterns when the divisor stays the same by recording the following problems and solutions on newsprint. For each problem, consider the context of markers and the context of brownies when recording each solution.

For example, $10 \div 3 = 3$ R1 (markers) and $3\frac{1}{3}$ (brownies).

$1 \div 3 =$	$1 \div 4 =$	$1 \div 5 =$	$1 \div 6 =$
$2 \div 3 =$	$2 \div 4 =$	$2 \div 5 =$	$2 \div 6 =$
$3 \div 3 =$	$3 \div 4 =$	$3 \div 5 =$	$3 \div 6 =$
$4 \div 3 =$	$4 \div 4 =$	$4 \div 5 =$	$4 \div 6 =$
$5 \div 3 =$	$5 \div 4 =$	$5 \div 5 =$	$5 \div 6 =$
$6 \div 3 =$	$6 \div 4 =$	$6 \div 5 =$	$6 \div 6 =$
$7 \div 3 =$	$7 \div 4 =$	$7 \div 5 =$	$7 \div 6 =$
$8 \div 3 =$	$8 \div 4 =$	$8 \div 5 =$	$8 \div 6 =$
$9 \div 3 =$	$9 \div 4 =$	$9 \div 5 =$	$9 \div 6 =$
$10 \div 3 =$	$10 \div 4 =$	$10 \div 5 =$	$10 \div 6 =$
$11 \div 3 =$	$11 \div 4 =$	$11 \div 5 =$	$11 \div 6 =$
$12 \div 3 =$	$12 \div 4 =$	$12 \div 5 =$	$12 \div 6 =$
$13 \div 3 =$	$13 \div 4 =$	$13 \div 5 =$	$13 \div 6 =$
$14 \div 3 =$	$14 \div 4 =$	$14 \div 5 =$	$14 \div 6 =$
$15 \div 3 =$	$15 \div 4 =$	$15 \div 5 =$	$15 \div 6 =$

Which dividends do not have remainders? What is the pattern?

____

Which dividends have a remainder of one? A remainder of 2? A remainder of 3, and so on? What patterns do you notice?

____

What is the largest remainder you found for your divisor? Why do you think this is so?

____

The Dividend Stays the Same

In this lesson, students interpret and solve several series of division problems in which the dividend stays the same and the divisors go from 1 to 10.

Investigating Patterns

Investigate patterns when the dividend stays the same by recording the following problems and solutions on newsprint. For each problem, consider the context of markers and the context of brownies when recording each solution.

For example, 2 ÷ 5 = 0 R2 (markers) and $\frac{2}{5}$ (brownies).

1 ÷ 1 =	2 ÷ 1 =	3 ÷ 1 =	4 ÷ 1 =
1 ÷ 2 =	2 ÷ 2 =	3 ÷ 2 =	4 ÷ 2 =
1 ÷ 3 =	2 ÷ 3 =	3 ÷ 3 =	4 ÷ 3 =
1 ÷ 4 =	2 ÷ 4 =	3 ÷ 4 =	4 ÷ 4 =
1 ÷ 5 =	2 ÷ 5 =	3 ÷ 5 =	4 ÷ 5 =
1 ÷ 6 =	2 ÷ 6 =	3 ÷ 6 =	4 ÷ 6 =
1 ÷ 7 =	2 ÷ 7 =	3 ÷ 7 =	4 ÷ 7 =
1 ÷ 8 =	2 ÷ 8 =	3 ÷ 8 =	4 ÷ 8 =
1 ÷ 9 =	2 ÷ 9 =	3 ÷ 9 =	4 ÷ 9 =
1 ÷ 10=	2 ÷ 10=	3 ÷ 10 =	4 ÷ 10 =
1 ÷ 11=	2 ÷ 11 =	3 ÷ 11 =	4 ÷ 11 =
1 ÷ 12=	2 ÷ 12 =	3 ÷ 12 =	4 ÷ 12 =
1 ÷ 13=	2 ÷ 13 =	3 ÷ 13 =	4 ÷ 13 =
1 ÷ 14=	2 ÷ 14 =	3 ÷ 14 =	4 ÷ 14 =
1 ÷ 15=	2 ÷ 15 =	3 ÷ 15 =	4 ÷ 15 =

When a quotient is represented as zero with a remainder, why are the remainder and the dividend the same?

____

When problems have the same dividend but different divisors, all of which are greater than that dividend, why do they all result in the same quotient—zero with a remainder that is the same as the dividend?

____

When a quotient is expressed as a fraction, for example, 5 ÷ 7 = , why are the dividend and the numerator the same? Why are the divisor and the denominator the same?

____

The Factor Game

The Factor Game gives students practice with basic division facts and increases their fluency, understanding of, and familiarity with the relationship between numbers and their factors.

Key Questions:

Materials
• recording sheet, 1 per pair of students

- When it is your turn to select a number, what number do you look for and why?
- Are there any numbers on the game board you try to avoid? Why?
- Which numbers have many factors? Which numbers are prime (have only two factors, one and itself)?

Game Directions:

1. List the numbers to be used, (1–15) or (1–30), on the top of the board.
2. Review the meaning of *factor* and tell students that in this game the object is to get more points than your partner. Explain the two ways points are scored in each round.
    - Select a number from the lists that is not yet crossed out and record it as your score for the round.
    - Find all the proper factors of the number your opponent selected that are not yet crossed out. The sum of those factors is your score for the round.
3. Display a copy of the recording sheet and model how to use it, listing the numbers to use at the top of the score sheet.
4. Player 1 selects a number from the list, crosses it off the list, and records the number on the score sheet as his or her score for that round.
5. Player 2 identifies all of the proper factors of Player 1's number that haven't yet been crossed out. (Proper factors are smaller than the selected number.) For each factor, Player 2 writes a division sentence to prove it's a factor and crosses it off the list. Player 2's score for the round is the total of the factors.

~~1~~ 2 ~~3~~ 4 ~~5~~ 6 7 8 9 ~~10~~
11 12 13 14 ~~15~~

Player 1		Player 2	
proof	score	score	proof
	15		
		5	$15 \div 3 = 5$
		3	$15 \div 5 = 3$
		1	$15 \div 15 = 1$
		9	
		10	
		19	

6. Player 2 selects a number from the list that isn't crossed out and that has at least one factor in the list that is not crossed out. Player 2 crosses off the selected number, records it on the score sheet, and finds his or her new total.
7. Player 1 repeats step 6. Players alternate turns until no more numbers from the list can be used.
8. Players write their scores and who won at the bottom of the score sheet.

Game Reflection Sheet

What important ideas about multiplication and division does this lesson address?	
What connections can you make to the Common Core State Standards?	
What questions will you ask to probe students' understanding?	
How could you modify or extend the activity?	

The Factor Game Recording Sheet

number list

proof	score	score	proof

________ had ________ points.

________ had ________ points.

________ wins by ________ points.

number list

proof	score	score	proof

________ had ________ points.

________ had ________ points.

________ wins by ________ points.

How Long? How Many?

This game provides experience with multiplication in a geometric context using Cuisenaire® rods. It reinforces the concept of equal groups in multiplication.

Key Questions

- I see you labeled that array ____ × ____. What do those numbers represent?
- What is the largest array that will still fit on your game board?
- How are you calculating the number of squares you have covered?

Materials

- Cuisenaire rods
- 1 die
- *How Long? How Many?* recording sheet, 1 per student

Game Directions

1. Each partner uses a different recording sheet.
2. On your turn, roll the die twice. The first roll tells how long a Cuisenaire rod to use. The second roll tells how many rods to take.
3. Arrange the rods into a rectangle. Trace it on your grid. Write the multiplication equation inside.
4. When one person is blocked and cannot place a rectangle because there is no room on the grid, the game is over
5. Figure out how many squares on your grid are covered and how many are uncovered. Check each other's answers.

How Long? How Many? Recording Sheet

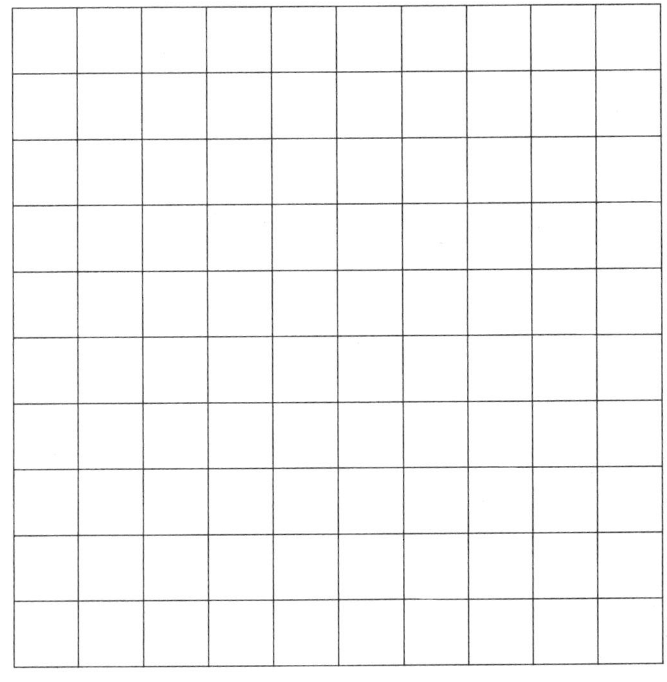

Covered _______

Uncovered _____

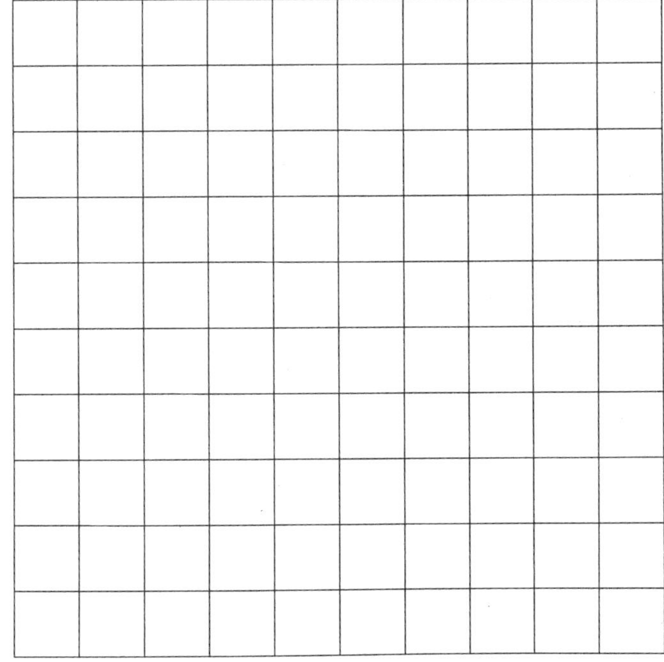

Covered _______

Uncovered _____

The Game of Leftovers

This game of chance gives students experience using the sharing model of division to divide quantities of color tiles into equal groups and think about remainders.

Key Questions

- What do the paper plates represent in the division equation?
- How do you determine how many color tiles (the quotient) to put on each plate?
- What is the significance of the remainder in this game?
- What number would you like to roll right now? Why?

Materials

- 1 die
- 15 color tiles
- 1 cup to hold tiles
- six 3-inch paper plates or paper squares

Game Directions

1. Take turns with your partner. On your turn, roll the die, take that number of paper plates or squares, and divide the tiles among them. Keep any leftover tiles.
2. Both players record the math sentence that describes what happened.

   For example: $15 \div 4 = 3$ R3

   In front of each sentence, write the initial of the person who rolled the die.
3. Return the tiles on the plates to the cup before the next player takes a turn.
4. Play until all the tiles are gone. Then, figure your scores by counting how many tiles each of you has. The winner is the player with the most leftovers. Add your scores to make sure that they total the 15 tiles you started with.

Leftovers With 100

This game provides students practice with division and gives them experience thinking about the significance of remainders. As students try to get large remainders, they focus on the relationship between divisors and dividends.

Key Questions

- How do you decide which divisors are good choices?
- At the end of a game, why does it make sense for the total of both your remainders to be 100?
- The new start number each time is the previous divisor times the answer without the remainder. Why does this make sense?

Materials

- Paper for recording sheet, 1 per student

Game Directions

1. Set up a recording sheet as shown.
2. Player 1 chooses a divisor from 1 to 20 and divides the start number, 100, by the divisor chosen. Player 2 records the division, crosses out the divisor, and circles and labels the remainder with Player 1's initial.

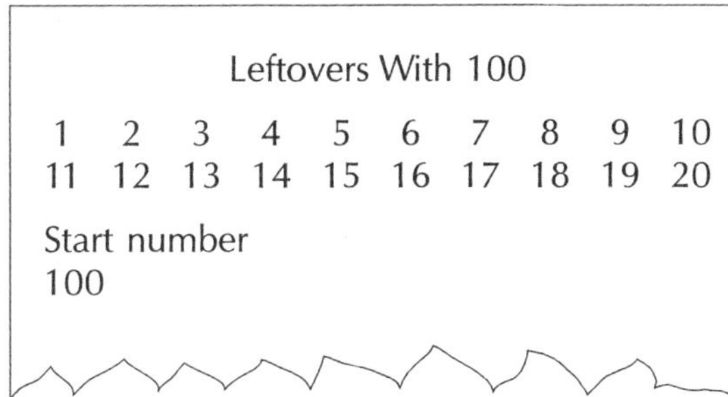

3. Both players subtract the remainder from the start number to get the next start number.
4. Player 2 uses the new start number, chooses a divisor that has not yet been crossed out, and divides. Divisors can only be used once. Player 1 records the division, crosses out the divisor, and circles and labels the remainder. Both players subtract the remainder from the start number to get the next start number.
5. Players continue taking turns until the start number reaches 0.

   Players add their remainders. The player with the larger sum wins.
6. Check that the sum of both players' remainders equals one hundred. If not, an error has been made.

Multiplication Bingo

This game gives students practice with multiplication facts. The game can be played with the whole class, or with a small group of students, and is easy to differentiate. Students enjoy the choices they have in creating their own cards.

Key Questions

- What is helpful to consider as you decide which products to write on your board?

Materials
• 2 dice per group of students
• Paper, 1 per student (grid paper optional)

Game Directions

1. Discuss the smallest and largest numbers possible from rolling two dice and multiplying the two numbers. Discuss which numbers between 1 and 36 are possible. Consider listing them on the board for students to reference.
2. Students create their game boards by recording a number in each square and an ✕ in the middle "free" square. It is okay to write numbers more than once.

		✕		

3. Roll the dice and announce the two numbers rolled. Students mark out the product of the two numbers on their boards. If the product appears on the board more than once, they only mark one of them.
4. Continue until someone gets a Bingo.
5. After children are familiar with the game, lead a discussion about how products can be made.
6. Note: For an alternate version students can play *Baby Bingo Blackout*. The game board is a 3-by-3 grid. There is no free space. The first student that marks out all 9 numbers on his or her board is the winner.

Hit the Target

This game provides opportunities to use estimation, a calculator, and mental computation. Students choose factors to multiply as they attempt to reach a targeted product in the fewest number of tries.

Key Questions

- Which numbers are difficult to start with and which are easy?
- What strategies are you using to calculate mentally?

Materials

- Calculator, 1 per pair of students
- Paper for recording

Game Directions

1. Players choose or are given a target range (800–850, for example), depending on the kinds of numbers they are comfortable with.
2. Player 1 chooses a number between 1 and 100 (50, for example).
3. Player 2 chooses another number to multiply the first number by, either mentally or with a calculator (50 x 10, for example), and player 1 verifies and records the result.
4. If the product does not hit within the target range, player 2 goes back to the original number and multiplies it by another number (again, either mentally or with a calculator), and player 1 verifies and records the result.
5. Players repeat step 4 until the product falls within the target range.
6. Players repeat the game, this time alternating roles.

Game Reflection Sheet

Game:	How Long? How Many?	The Game of Leftovers
What important ideas about multiplication and division does this lesson address?		
What connections can you make to the Common Core State Standards?		
What questions will you ask to probe students' understanding?		
How could you modify or extend the activity?		

Game Reflection Sheet *(continued)*

Game:	Leftovers With 100	Multiplication Bingo
What important ideas about multiplication and division does this lesson address?		
What connections can you make to the Common Core State Standards?		
What questions will you ask to probe students' understanding?		
How could you modify or extend the activity?		

Game Reflection Sheet *(continued)*

Game:	Hit the Target	Additional Game
What important ideas about multiplication and division does this lesson address?		
What connections can you make to the Common Core State Standards?		
What questions will you ask to probe students' understanding?		
How could you modify or extend the activity?		

Developing Arithmetic Understanding

The Common Core State Standards call for computation using strategies based on place value, properties of operations, and/or the relationship between operations.

Mathematical Properties

Mathematical properties, together with the operations of addition, subtraction, multiplication, and division, are the foundation of arithmetic. We use mathematical properties when performing computations and recalling basic facts. They can reduce the complexity of equations and expressions and aid in performing mental calculations more easily. Mathematical properties are an avenue to higher-level thinking because they illustrate general cases and can lead to mathematical generalizations.

Properties of Operations	Example
Associative property of addition	$(a + b) + c = a + (b + c)$
Commutative property of addition	$a + b = b + a$
Additive identity property of 0	$a + 0 = 0 + a = a$
Existence of additive inverses	For every a there exists $-a$ so that $a + (-a) = (-a) + a = 0$
Associative property of multiplication	$(a \times b) \times c = a \times (b \times c)$
Commutative property of multiplication	$a \times b = b \times a$
Multiplicative identity property of 1	$a \times 1 = 1 \times a = a$
Existence of multiplicative inverses	For every $a \neq 0$ there exists $1/a$ so that $a \times 1/a = 1/a \times a = 1$
Distributive property of multiplication over addition	$a \times (b + c) = a \times b + a \times c$

True or False? Task

1. Place the pile of number sentences face down. Turn over the top number sentence.
2. First think alone, and then discuss with your partner the following questions:
   - Is the sentence true or false?
   - How do you know?
   - Is your explanation the same or different than your partner's?
3. Place the number sentence in either the true or false pile.
4. Continue sorting and talking about each number sentence.

Open Sentences Task

1. Cut out the numbers so that they can easily be moved while discussing solutions.
2. Work with a partner to determine what number can be placed in the box to make the open sentence a true sentence.
3. As you and your partner work to complete the task, talk about the following:
   - How does the placement of the box or variable influence the complexity of an open sentence?
   - What might you learn about a child's understanding from this experience?

True, False, and Open Sentences Task

1. Order the set of mathematical sentences from *a* to *t* and put the labels *Always True*, *Never True*, and *Sometimes True* in the center of the table.
2. With your partner, examine the mathematical sentences, one at a time, and decide how to categorize them by answering the following question:
   - Is it always true, never true, or sometimes true? Explain.
3. When you have sorted all the mathematical sentences, compare your results with the other set of partners at your table. Discuss any discrepancies.

True or False Number Sentences

a.	b.
$3 \times 7 = 7 + 7 + 7$	$6 \times 4 = 4 + 4 + 4 + 4$
c.	d.
$7 \times 8 = (2 \times 8) + (5 \times 8)$	$8 \times 6 = 8 \times 5 + 6$
e.	f.
$9 \times 7 = 10 \times 7 - 7$	$9 + 6 = 10 + 5$
g.	h.
$37 + 56 = 39 + 54$	$33 - 27 = 34 - 26$
i.	j.
$93 = 9 + 30$	$94 = 80 + 14$

Open Sentences

a. $8 + 7 = \square + 6$

b. $8 \times 7 = \square \times 7 + 7$

c. $18 + 22 = 32 + \square$

d. $\square = 12$

e. $8 + 7 = 15 + \square$

f. $10 + 8 + \square = 12 + 9$

g. $\square + 15 + 25 = 17 + 28$

h. $73 + 56 = 71 + 59 - \square$

i. $12 \div 4 = [8 \div \square] + [4 \div \square]$

j. $66 \div \square = (60 \div 6) + 1$

0	1	2	3	4	5	6
7	8	9	10	11	12	13

True, False, and Open Sentences

Always True	Sometimes True	Never True

a. $0 \times 2 = \square \times 0$

b. $3 + \square = \square + 3$

c. $15 - 7 = 16 - 8$

d. $2 \times \square = \square + \square + \square$

e. $\square \times 9 = (\square \times 10) - (\square \times 1)$

f. $89 = \square + 80$

g. $\square = 1 \times \square$

h. $16 \div 8 = 8 \div 16$

i. $\square \times 0 = 0$

j. $8 + 2 = 3 + 8$

True, False, and Open Sentences

(continued)

k. 12 = 12	**l.** 24 ÷ 2 = □ + 3
m. 1 ÷ □ x □ = 1	**n.** (5 x 6) x □ = (5 x □) x 6
o. 8 + 5 = □ + 8	**p.** □ x 12 = (□ x 10) + (□ x 2)
q. 15 – 7 = 7 – 15	**r.** □ = □ + 0
s. (5 – 3) – 1 = 5 – (3 – 1)	**t.** 0 = □ – □

Procedural Fluency: Alternative Algorithms

To cultivate procedural fluency, it is important to focus students on developing accuracy and efficiency with procedures through understanding. Learning procedures through understanding results in better retention and fewer errors.

You Try It!

Mentally solve the problem below and record your strategy below.

28 × 6 =

Reviewing Student Responses

Examine the sample work and consider whether the strategies are based on place value, the relationship between addition and subtraction, the relationship between multiplication and division, or properties of operations.

Adbram's Work

28
× 6
6x8 = 48
6x20 = 120
168
28x6 = (30x3)+(30x3) - 12 = 168
25x6 = 150 + 18 = 168
Since 25 is easy becau[se] of quarters, I change 28 to 25. (25·6) Which equals 150 +(6×3)=168. The reason I did that was because 28-3=25.

Sabine's Work

Multiplacation

$$\begin{array}{r} 28 \\ \times\ 6 \\ \hline \end{array}$$

28x2=56
28x2= 56
28x2= 56
168

$$\begin{array}{r} 28 \\ \times\ 6 \\ \hline \end{array} \qquad \begin{array}{r} 56 \\ +28 \\ \hline 84 \end{array}$$

28x3=(56+28)=84
28x3=84
168

Brendan's Work

$$\begin{array}{r} 28 \\ \times 6 \\ \hline 48 \\ +120 \\ \hline 168 \end{array}$$

30×6=180−12=168

Margaret's Work

28×6=168
8×6=48
6×20=120
168

28×3=84
28×3=84
+
168

Tell Me All You Can

This routine encourages students to think and communicate about equations before solving them. In addition to developing number sense, this activity promotes efficient test-taking skills as students are encouraged to consider reasonableness.

1. Record an open equation on the board (e.g., 562 − 237 = ____).
2. Ask students to tell you what they know about the problem (not the answer).
3. Have students prove their conjectures with mathematical explanations.
4. Have students solve the problem and explain their strategies.

Key Questions

- What do you know about this problem?
- Is the answer going to be more or less than ____? How do you know?

Sentence Frames

The answer is going to be about ____ because ____.

The answer is going to be between ____ and ____ because ____.

The answer is going to be less than ____ because ____.

The answer is going to be greater than ____ because ____.

Reflection: Algorithms and Procedural Fluency

1. How can you foster students' understanding and flexibility with algorithms?

____

____

2. What are some changes or shifts that you believe will be important in developing the type of procedural fluency that is expected by the Common Core State Standards?

____

____

____

Promoting Decimal Sense

Students have increased number sense with decimals when they can use mathematical representations flexibly and translate among different models.

Decimal Concepts

Students often think a "decimal" is the decimal point rather than a number. It is important that students understand that the decimal point is a symbol that indicates the location of the ones place and all other subsequent places in the decimal system. The ideas of whole-number place value extend to decimals. Students can often name a specific place in the decimal system—tenths, hundredths—but may not understand the value of that place. If students do not understand the relationship between place value (that 0.6 is 10 times larger than 0.06, for example) or realize that the place value can be represented using other place values (13 tenths is equal to 130 hundredths), they will have great difficulty with decimal numbers.

Models to Support Understanding

Decimal concepts are often presented to students using symbols. However, physical models that represent the quantities and the multiplicative relationships between place values can help individuals make sense of these ideas.

Base Ten Blocks

Models such as base ten blocks can be used to help students develop an understanding of the numbers that are represented by decimal notation.

Number Line

The number line is a model that presents decimal fractions as measures or distances from zero.

Recent cognitive research seems to indicate that using a variety of models and explicitly asking students to focus on the underlying similarities among models help them generalize important ideas.

Identifying Aspects of Learning

Math learning relies on making sense of logical structures as well as learning social conventions. Identifying whether the math content you are teaching is logical or social knowledge will help create appropriate learning experiences.

Two Aspects of Learning Mathematics

Teaching *social knowledge* requires providing the learner with information—direct instruction, or teaching by telling, is essential. The appropriate pedagogical choice for teaching *logical knowledge* is to provide the learner with opportunities to interact with new ideas in order to bring meaning to those ideas. In this instance, the source of the knowledge and the process of developing understanding are internal to the learner.

Aspects of Learning Mathematics	
Learning Social Conventions: Social Knowledge	**Making Sense: Logical Knowledge**
The source of the learning is external.	*The source of the learning is internal.*
• Knowing which symbols to use to represent ideas • Understanding the words people use to talk about mathematical ideas	• Reasoning about mathematics • Constructing mathematical arguments • Using prior understanding to construct new knowledge

Focus and coherence in the Standards provide the time that students need to make sense of *logical knowledge*. Teachers no longer need to feel the pressure to try to teach *logical knowledge* by telling or by resorting to mnemonic devices or tricks in order to cover the curriculum, but can teach for the level of rigor required in the Standards.

Reflection: Teaching Mathematics

What aspects of decimals do students need to make sense of for themselves?

Connecting Multiple Representations

Mathematical representations support student learning by making abstract concepts concrete for all students.

Types of Representations

According to *Principles and Standards for School Mathematics* (NCTM, 2000), the use of representations is critical to students' understanding of mathematical concepts and relationships. Students can use representations to clarify and communicate mathematical approaches, arguments, and understandings. Mathematical representations are interconnected and can be varied, from written symbols and equations to graphs and real-life situations.

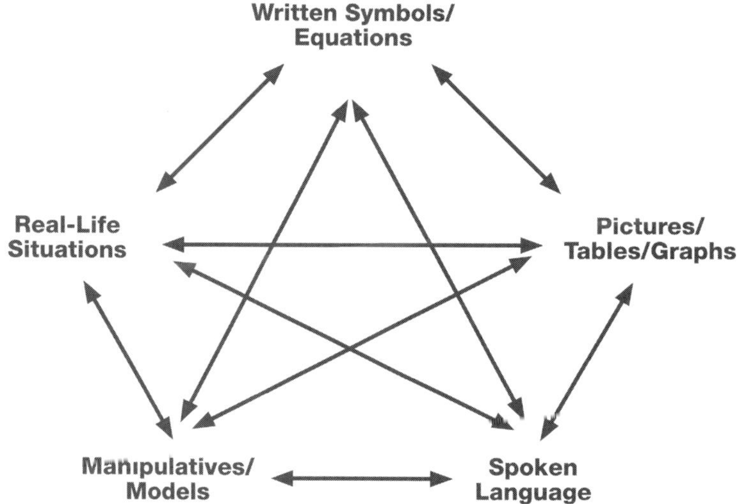

Reflection: Considering Multiple Representations

1. What does this focus on multiple representations bring to mind as you consider your teaching practice?

 ____

 ____

2. What can you do to foster students' ability to use tools and representations?

 ____

 ____

Small 10-by-10 Grids

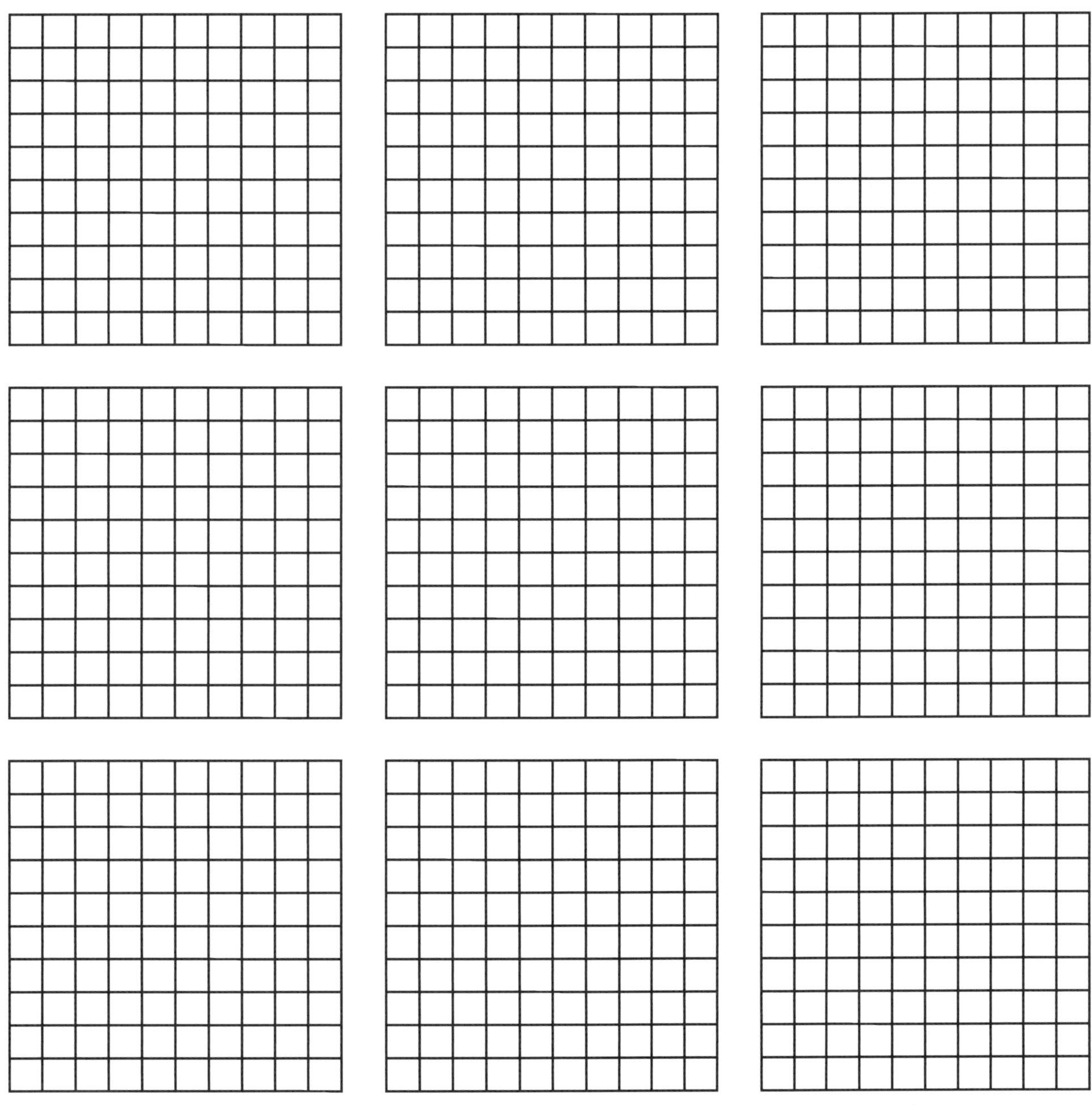

Decimal Representations
Recording Sheet

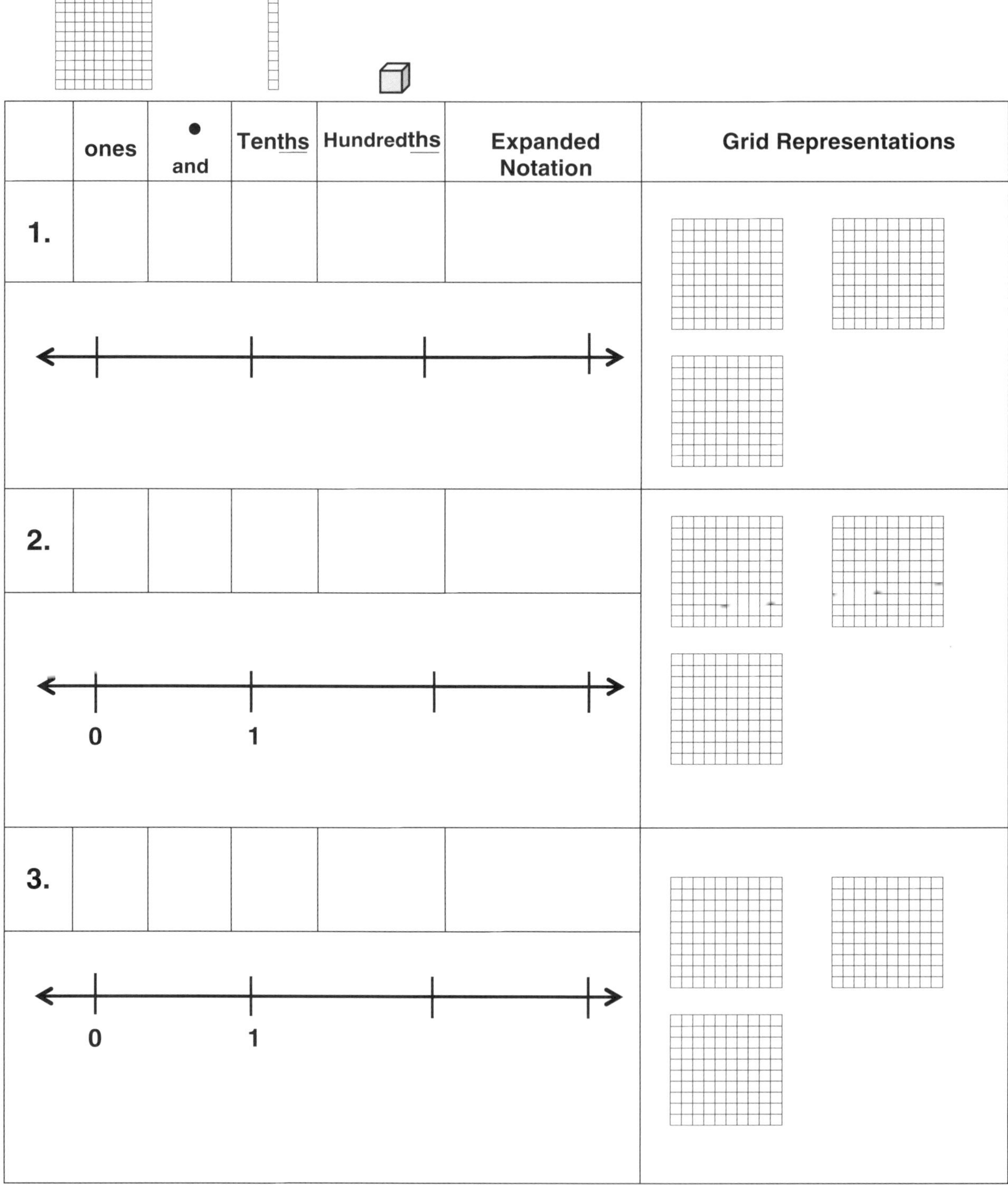

	ones	• and	Tenths	Hundredths	Expanded Notation	Grid Representations
1.						
2.						
3.						

Learning From Student Work

Making assessment an integral part of instruction is essential for improving the effectiveness of math instruction.

Multiple Strategies

How could you find the answer to 23 × 4 on a calculator if the 4 button is broken? Record two different ways below the problem.

Ben's Work

23 × 4

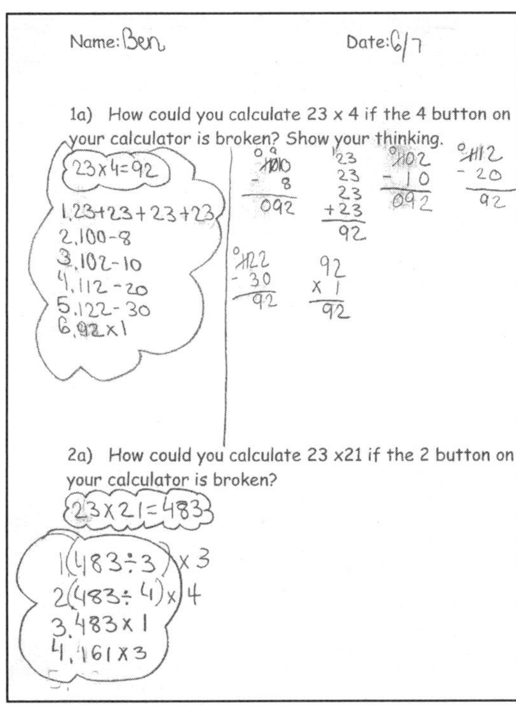
Name: Ben Date: 6/7

1a) How could you calculate 23 x 4 if the 4 button on your calculator is broken? Show your thinking.

23x4=92

1. 23+23+23+23
2. 100-8
3. 102-10
4. 112-20
5. 122-30
6. 92x1

2a) How could you calculate 23 x21 if the 2 button on your calculator is broken?

23x21=483

1. (483÷3) x 3
2. (483÷4) x 4
3. 483x1
4. 161x3

Reviewing Student Strategies

Use the three-column T-chart that was introduced to record your thinking about each student's strategies.

What I See	What I Infer From What I See	Questions About What I Infer

Kirsten's Work

Name: Kirsten Date: June 7.

1a) How could you calculate 23 x 4 if the 4 button on your calculator is broken? Show your thinking.

most simple	most efficent	algebratic
(23x2)x2=92	23x 2= 46 +23x 2= 46 23x4= 92	(23x3)+23

Ⓐ My answer is 92 because when you can't use the 4 for 23x4 you could do (23x3)+23 because you would have 4 groups of 23.

2a) How could you calculate 23 x21 if the 2 button on your calculator is broken?

① (13x10) x(10x11)=240

② (10+10+3) x(10+10+1) = 240

③ (11.5+11.5)x(10.5x10.5) = 240 * my favorite

Ⓐ My answer is 240 because you can do (11.5+11.5)x(10.5+10.5) = 240 Ⓐ

What I See	What I Infer From What I See	Questions About What I Infer

Rohan's Work

Name: Rohan Date: 6-7

1a) How could you calculate 23 x 4 if the 4 button on your calculator is broken? Show your thinking.

I used the factors of 4 since the 4 key is busted, the factors were 1, 2, and 4, since the 4 key is busted 4x1 won't work so 1 and 4 are crossed out, so 2 is left. 2x2 is 4 so is use 2x2x23 for my answer.

23x2x2=92
23x4=92

2a) How could you calculate 23 x21 if the 2 button on your calculator is broken?

I used the exact same strategy as the last problem exeept this time I used 21's factors. They are 1, 3, 7, 21, 1 and 21 are crossed out since 1x21 has a two in it so 3x7=21. Then 3x7x= addents of 23, so I just used 19+4,

19+4 x 3x7 =483
23x21=483

What I See	What I Infer From What I See	Questions About What I Infer

Reflection: Linking Assessment and Instruction

1. What are two ideas that have made an impact on your thinking about assessment?

____

____

____

Mind Map

Create a Mind Map addressing the big ideas of coherence, focus, and rigor as well as the implications for teaching and learning.

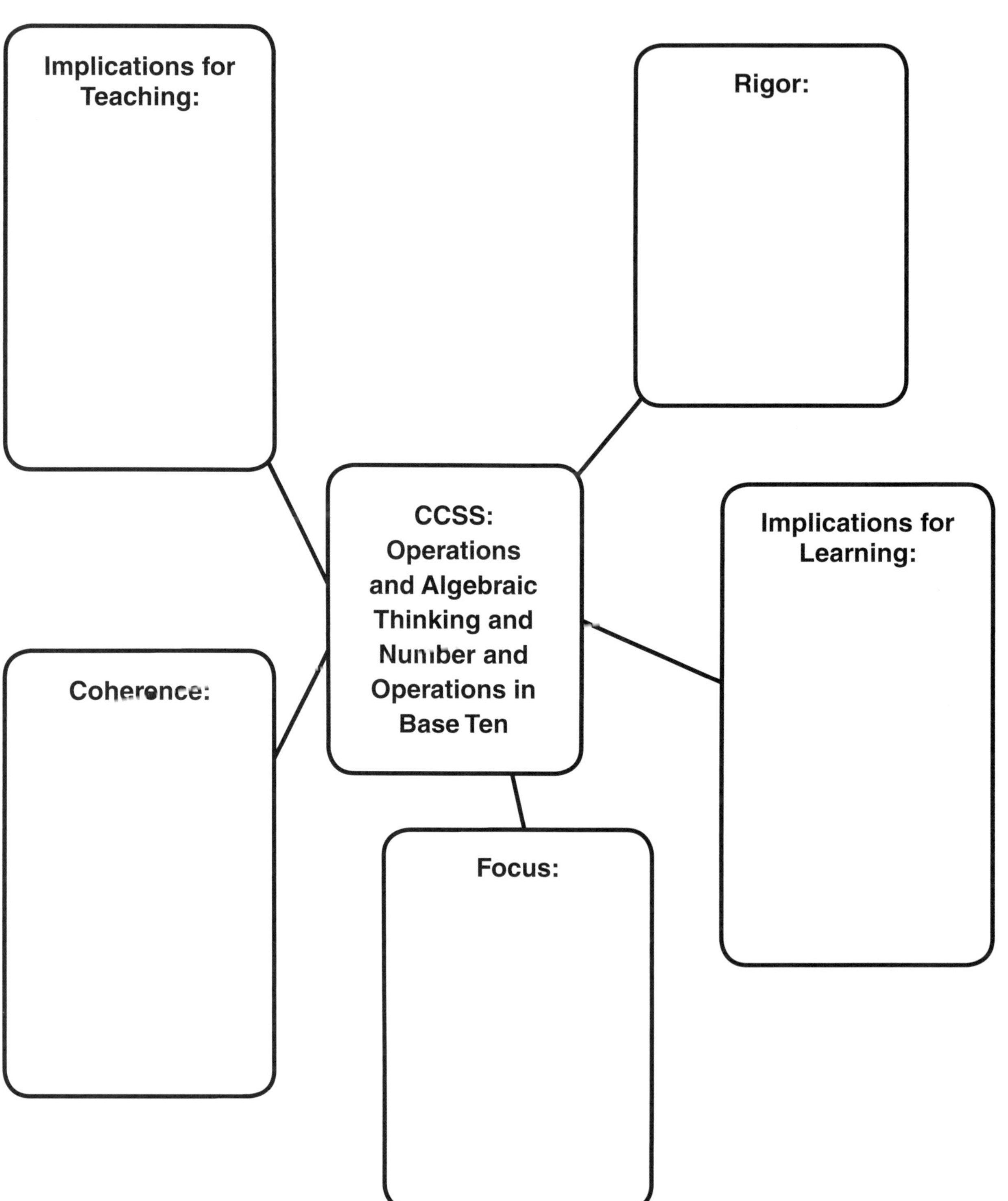

Session Resources

Professional Article: Linking Assessment and Instruction

By Marilyn Burns

Making assessment an integral part of instruction is essential for improving the effectiveness of classroom math instruction. When learning math in school, we all experienced doing assignments and taking quizzes to give our teachers information about how we were doing. Typically, these assignments and quizzes called for performing calculations and solving problems with the focus on getting right answers. And while assignments and quizzes are useful vehicles for measuring students' progress, and correct answers are important, merely checking whether or not answers are correct is insufficient. Assessments must also uncover what students understand and provide insights into how they think and reason. Key to assessing students' math learning is to delve into how students arrive at answers.

To accomplish this, assessment must play an integral role in classroom instruction, not only to monitor individual students' progress but also to reflect on our teaching to maximize the effectiveness of our lessons. After teaching a lesson, it is helpful to ask:

What did the students learn? If I teach the same grade level next year, should I repeat this lesson? Should I make changes to it? If I decide not to repeat the lesson, how might I rethink what I was trying to accomplish? This continual evaluation of instructional choices is at the heart of both monitoring student progress and improving our teaching practice.

Posing questions is an effective instructional tool for stimulating students' thinking. It is also an essential assessment tool for uncovering what students understand. It is important to consider the kinds of questions, both oral and written, that serve to provide insights into how students think. When we ask a question that calls for a correct response, we need to broaden our listening focus so that we don't listen merely for the correct answer (that we hope to hear) but also push further to listen to the reasoning behind the answer. And while it's typical to probe students when they give an incorrect answer, it is just as important to probe them when their answers are correct. Correct answers can mask confusion.

Here is an example. Fourth graders were asked to write five fractions in order from least to greatest—$\frac{1}{4}$, $\frac{11}{16}$, $\frac{3}{8}$, $\frac{1}{16}$, $\frac{3}{4}$. They were also asked to write about their reasons for ordering the fractions. After they had time to solve the problem, they participated in a whole-class discussion. Robert reported first. He said with confidence, and correctly, "The smallest fraction is one-sixteenth." When asked to explain how he knew that $\frac{1}{16}$ was the smallest fraction, Robert read from his paper, again with confidence, "Because one-sixteenth is the lowest number in fractions."

The students had previously cut and labeled strips of construction paper to make the fraction kits, and $\frac{1}{16}$ happened to be the smallest piece in their kits. The fraction kit—a standard and effective instructional tool—had led Robert to an incorrect generalization. Requiring that Robert give more than the correct answer, but also the reasoning behind it, unveiled his misconception. This experience called for not only dealing with Robert but also rethinking how to use the fraction kit so that students would understand that we could cut smaller and smaller fraction pieces and find fraction names for even the tiniest sliver.

Incorporating students' reasoning into both written assignments and classroom discussions is a crucial step toward making assessment an integral and ongoing aspect of classroom instruction. It should be a staple of math teaching.

Assessment Through Students' Written Work

One main strategy for assessing students' learning is to incorporate writing into math assignments. There are many ways to present writing assignments that yield information about how students are thinking. Here are four strategies.

Ask for more than one strategy.
Solving math problems often requires making false starts and searching for new approaches. Students need to develop multiple strategies so that they become flexible in their mathematical thinking and are able to look at mathematical situations from different perspectives. Even when students are performing routine computations, asking them to demonstrate more than one way to arrive at an answer provides insight into their thinking.

Let students set parameters.

A good technique for assessing students' understanding, as well as differentiating instruction, is to make an assignment adjustable in some way, so that it is accessible and appropriate for a wide range of students. For example, asking students to write their own word problems, and solve them, can give you information about their numerical comfort as well as their computational skills.

Assess the same concept or skill in different ways.

Students' beginning understanding, although fragile, can provide useful building blocks or connections to more robust learning. Sometimes a familiar context can help a student think about a numerically challenging problem. Using flexible assessment approaches enables us to build on students' strengths and interests and help them move on from there.

Take occasional class inventories.

Compiling an inventory from a set of papers can provide a sense of the class's progress and thus inform decisions about how to differentiate instruction. For example, after students complete an assignment that includes having them explain their reasoning, review their papers and list the strategies they used. Use this information to inform future lessons and for providing intervention for the struggling students.

Assessment Through Classroom Discussion

Incorporating assessment into classroom discussion serves two goals: it provides insights into students' thinking, and it insures that no student is invisible in the class—that all are participating and working to understand and learn. Try the following strategies.

Ask students to explain their answers, whether or not the answers are correct.

Follow up on both correct and incorrect answers by asking students to explain their reasoning. While you know the correct answer, avoid having a preconceived response about how a student should have reasoned. Students can arrive at correct answers in unexpected ways. For example, Brandon, a fifth grader, when comparing $\frac{4}{5}$ and $\frac{3}{4}$, changed the fractions so that they had common numerators: $\frac{12}{15}$ and $\frac{12}{16}$. He knew that sixteenths were smaller than fifteenths, so $\frac{12}{15}$ or $\frac{4}{5}$ had to be larger.

Ask students to share their solution strategies with the class.

After a student responds to a question and explains his or her reasoning, ask, "Who has a different way to solve the problem?" or "Who has another way to think about this?" Provide sufficient wait time to encourage students to collect their thoughts. In addition to providing insights into students' thinking and understanding, this method reinforces the idea that there are different ways to think about problems and lets the students know that you value their individual approaches.

Call on students who don't volunteer.

Let your students know that it's important for you to learn about how each of them thinks and, for that reason, to hear from all of them. Reassure them, however, that if you call on them and they don't know the answer, they should just let you know, because that is valuable information that will help you think about the support they need.

Use small-group work.

This technique is especially useful for drawing out students who are reticent about talking in front of the whole class. After posing a problem, say, "Turn and talk with your partner," or "Talk with your group about this." Then eavesdrop, paying especially close attention to the students that do not typically talk in class discussions.

Improving Mathematics Teaching

As stated in NCTM's Principles and Standards, "To ensure deep, high-quality learning for all students, assessment and instruction must be integrated so that assessment becomes a routine part of the ongoing classroom activity rather than an interruption. Such assessment also provides the information teachers need to make appropriate instructional decisions."

Making assessment an integral part of daily mathematics instruction is a challenge. It requires planning specific ways to use assignments and discussions to discover what students do and do not understand. It also requires teachers to be prepared to deal with students' responses. Merely spotting when students are incorrect is relatively easy compared with understanding the reasons behind their errors. The latter demands careful attention and a deep knowledge of the mathematics concepts that students are learning.

The benefits are worth the effort. By building and using a wide repertoire of assessment strategies, we can get to know more about our students than we ever thought possible. The insights we gain by making assessment a regular part of instruction enable us to meet the needs of the students who are eager for more challenges and to provide intervention for those who are struggling.

Professional Article: How Children Learn Mathematics

By Marilyn Burns

For learning to occur, three conditions are necessary: maturity, physical experience, and social interaction. The process of equilibration coordinates these three conditions.

Maturity

The older children are, the more likely their mental structures will act in coordinated ways. Young children shown a group of objects frequently claim there are a greater number when the objects are spread out, but older children no longer make this error. Younger children report what they perceive; older children have reached a level of mental maturity that allows them to understand that the number of objects does not change when the objects are repositioned. A child who does not see the contradiction between perception and reality is in a state of disequilibrium.

Physical experience

The more experiences children have with physical objects in the environment, the more likely related understanding will develop. Firsthand experimentation is needed. Merely looking at a soft drink can does not reveal the relationship between its height and its circumference. Testing an idea with physical materials provides valuable feedback for understanding relationships.

Social interaction

The more opportunities children have to interact with peers, parents, and teachers, the more they hear other viewpoints that help them gain perspective on their own ideas. Social interaction stimulates children to think through their own ideas and to approach objectivity. This type of interaction is also an important source of information about social customs and conventions.

What are the teaching implications for these conditions for learning? Essential to making instructional decisions is to consider the source of the learning of any new concept or skill. Mathematics relies on logical structures, and learning mathematics calls for making sense of these structures, for thinking, reasoning, and searching to uncover meaning. Learning mathematical ideas is all about sense making, and the source of the knowledge is internal; that is, it lies inside the learner.

Social knowledge, however, is also an aspect of mathematics. The symbolism that we use to represent ideas—the numerals we write to represent quantities and the symbols that we use to describe relationships—are social conventions that help us communicate about mathematical ideas. Because of this, the source of knowledge for vocabulary and symbols is external; that is, it lies outside the learner. It is not possible to figure out through reasoning or through searching to uncover meaning that the numbers we multiply are called factors and the answer to a multiplication problem is called a product, or that we use a symbol that looks like a period when expressing decimal numerals, for example, 5.76. These are arbitrary, agreed-upon conventions. The sources for learning social convention can be other people, books, TV shows, movies, or other sources outside the child.

For both types of knowledge—social and logical—explicit instruction is essential. However, the character of the instruction vastly differs. For teaching social knowledge, the correct, and really only, pedagogical choice is to provide the information to the learner, that is, to teach by telling or give the learner access to the information from another resource—a book, a magazine, a video—always drawing from a source of knowledge that is external to the learner. There's no way to figure out, for example, that numbers that aren't divisible by two are called odd numbers—we have to acquire knowledge of the terminology from an outside source. However, knowing if a specific number is or isn't divisible by two calls for understanding the characteristics of numbers that do and don't have a remainder of one when divided by two—we have to acquire this mathematical knowledge by making sense, synthesizing what we know about division, and connecting this understanding with what we know about patterns of numbers. For teaching logical knowledge, the appropriate pedagogical choice is to provide the learner with opportunities to interact with the ideas with the goal of bringing meaning to them— the source of the knowledge and the process of developing understanding are internal to the learner.

It's long been held as a true notion that you know something best when you teach it. Teaching in this context is typically thought of as explaining, with the goal of making concepts clear. In order to be able to explain an idea, you have to think it through for yourself first, understand it, and come up with some sort of sequence for presenting it. The process of preparing to teach in this way calls for sense making on the part of the teacher. While teachers always need to make sense of the mathematics they teach, the challenge is to find ways for the students to make sense for themselves so that they can connect new ideas to existing mental constructs in order to develop understanding of new ideas.

A teacher, another child, or a book can set a child in a direction for learning, offer some useful information, or explain an idea, but children have to construct understanding for themselves in order to make sense of mathematics. Rather than teaching by telling, teachers must structure learning activities that make use of physical materials, allow for social interaction, and provide opportunities for children to think, reason, and make sense of mathematics. You cannot talk a child into learning or tell a child to understand.

Collect Ten Recording Sheet

Name: ________________

Directions

1. For each pair of cards you collect, write the number of the first card in the first blank, then write the number of the second card in the second blank.
2. Finally, fill in the sum in the third blank.
3. At the end of the game, complete the sentence frames at the bottom of the page.

1.	_____ + _____ = _____	10.	_____ + _____ = _____
2.	_____ + _____ = _____	11.	_____ + _____ = _____
3.	_____ + _____ = _____	12.	_____ + _____ = _____
4.	_____ + _____ = _____	13.	_____ + _____ = _____
5.	_____ + _____ = _____	14.	_____ + _____ = _____
6.	_____ + _____ = _____	15.	_____ + _____ = _____
7.	_____ + _____ = _____	16.	_____ + _____ = _____
8.	_____ + _____ = _____	17.	_____ + _____ = _____
9.	_____ + _____ = _____	18.	_____ + _____ = _____

My total for *Collect Ten* is ________.

My total of ________ is ________ than my partner's total of ________.

Sums of More Than Ten Recording Sheet

Name: ____________________

Directions

1. Turn over the top *Sums of More Than Ten* card in your pile and record the number sentence.
2. Use counters to build the number sentence on your double ten-frame.
3. Make a ten by rearranging the counters you've placed and record the new number sentence.
4. Figure out the sum. Record the sum for both sentences.

1. ____________ + ____________ = ____________ + ____________

____________ = ____________

2. ____________ + ____________ = ____________ + ____________

____________ = ____________

3. ____________ + ____________ = ____________ + ____________

____________ = ____________

4. ____________ + ____________ = ____________ + ____________

____________ = ____________

(continued)

Sums of More Than Ten Recording Sheet *(continued)*

5. ________ + ________ = ________ + ________

________ = ________

6. ________ + ________ = ________ + ________

________ = ________

7. ________ + ________ = ________ + ________

________ = ________

8. ________ + ________ = ________ + ________

________ = ________

9. ________ + ________ = ________ + ________

________ = ________

10. ________ + ________ = ________ + ________

________ = ________

Spill and Compare Recording Sheet

Names: ______________________________ Our Number [ ]

More Reds	More Yellows	The Same Number of Reds and Yellows

Names: ______________________________ Our Number [ ]

More Reds	More Yellows	The Same Number of Reds and Yellows

Scaffolding the Open Number Line

Scaffolding Students' Experiences With the Open Number Line

The open number line is a computational tool for addition and subtraction that provides students with a visual model that is useful for building understanding and skills.

Some students may need explicit instruction helping them build on their prior experiences with the hundred chart.

What does the ___ stand for?

What does the + ___ stand for?

What does the ___ stand for?

I collected ___ acorns.

Then I collected ____ more.

How many acorns do I have?

1-100 Chart

1	2	3	4	5	6	7	8	9	10
11	12	13	14	15	16	17	18	19	20
21	22	23	24	25	26	27	28	29	30
31	32	33	34	35	36	37	38	39	40
41	42	43	44	45	46	47	48	49	50
51	52	53	54	55	56	57	58	59	60
61	62	63	64	65	66	67	68	69	70
71	72	73	74	75	76	77	78	79	80
81	82	83	84	85	86	87	88	89	90
91	92	93	94	95	96	97	98	99	100

Open Number Line
Equation

Scaffolding the Open Number Line

(continued)

I picked ___ apples.

Then I picked ____ more.

How many apples do I have?

1-100 Chart

1	2	3	4	5	6	7	8	9	10
11	12	13	14	15	16	17	18	19	20
21	22	23	24	25	26	27	28	29	30
31	32	33	34	35	36	37	38	39	40
41	42	43	44	45	46	47	48	49	50
51	52	53	54	55	56	57	58	59	60
61	62	63	64	65	66	67	68	69	70
71	72	73	74	75	76	77	78	79	80
81	82	83	84	85	86	87	88	89	90
91	92	93	94	95	96	97	98	99	100

Open Number Line
Equation

1-100 Chart

1	2	3	4	5	6	7	8	9	10
11	12	13	14	15	16	17	18	19	20
21	22	23	24	25	26	27	28	29	30
31	32	33	34	35	36	37	38	39	40
41	42	43	44	45	46	47	48	49	50
51	52	53	54	55	56	57	58	59	60
61	62	63	64	65	66	67	68	69	70
71	72	73	74	75	76	77	78	79	80
81	82	83	84	85	86	87	88	89	90
91	92	93	94	95	96	97	98	99	100

Open Number Line
Equation

101 and Out Recording Sheet

The game and recording method are modeled in this session. Note that the first example of "Equation" below starts on 1 because players start with 1 on the Hundred Chart used in this game.

Players take turns for up to 6 rolls each.

1. Roll the cube and record it.
2. Decide whether to use the roll as tens or ones. Add with an open number line.
3. Write an addition equation. Write the sum as your next starting number.

The winner is the player whose total is closer to 100. A player who goes over 100 is out!

Roll	Open Number Line	Equation
Roll 1 ____		1 + ____ = ____
Roll 2 ____		
Roll 3 ____		
Roll 4 ____		
Roll 5 ____		
Roll 6 ____		

Final Score:

The Factor Game Recording Sheet

number list				number list			
proof	score	score	proof	proof	score	score	proof

_______ had _______ points.

_______ had _______ points.

_______ wins by _______ points.

_______ had _______ points.

_______ had _______ points.

_______ wins by _______ points.

How Long? How Many? Recording Sheet

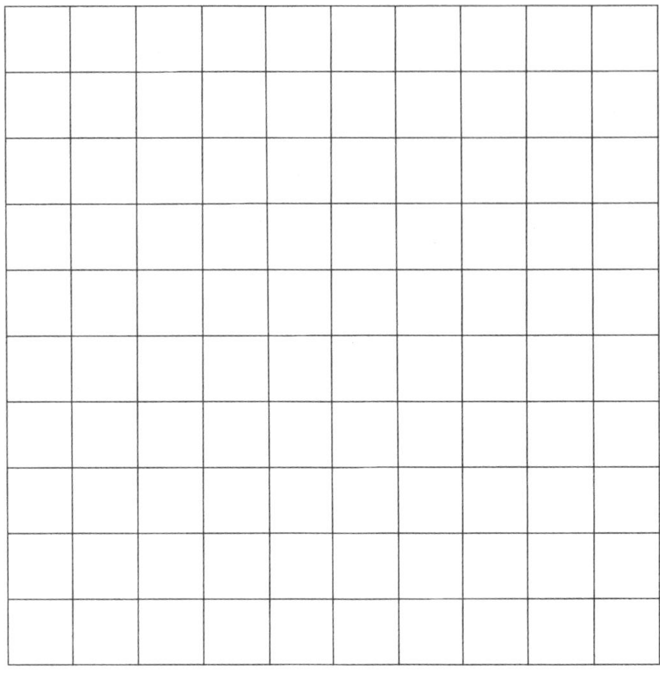

Covered _______

Uncovered _____

Covered _______

Uncovered _____

$\frac{1}{2}$-inch Grid Paper

Small 10-by-10 Grids

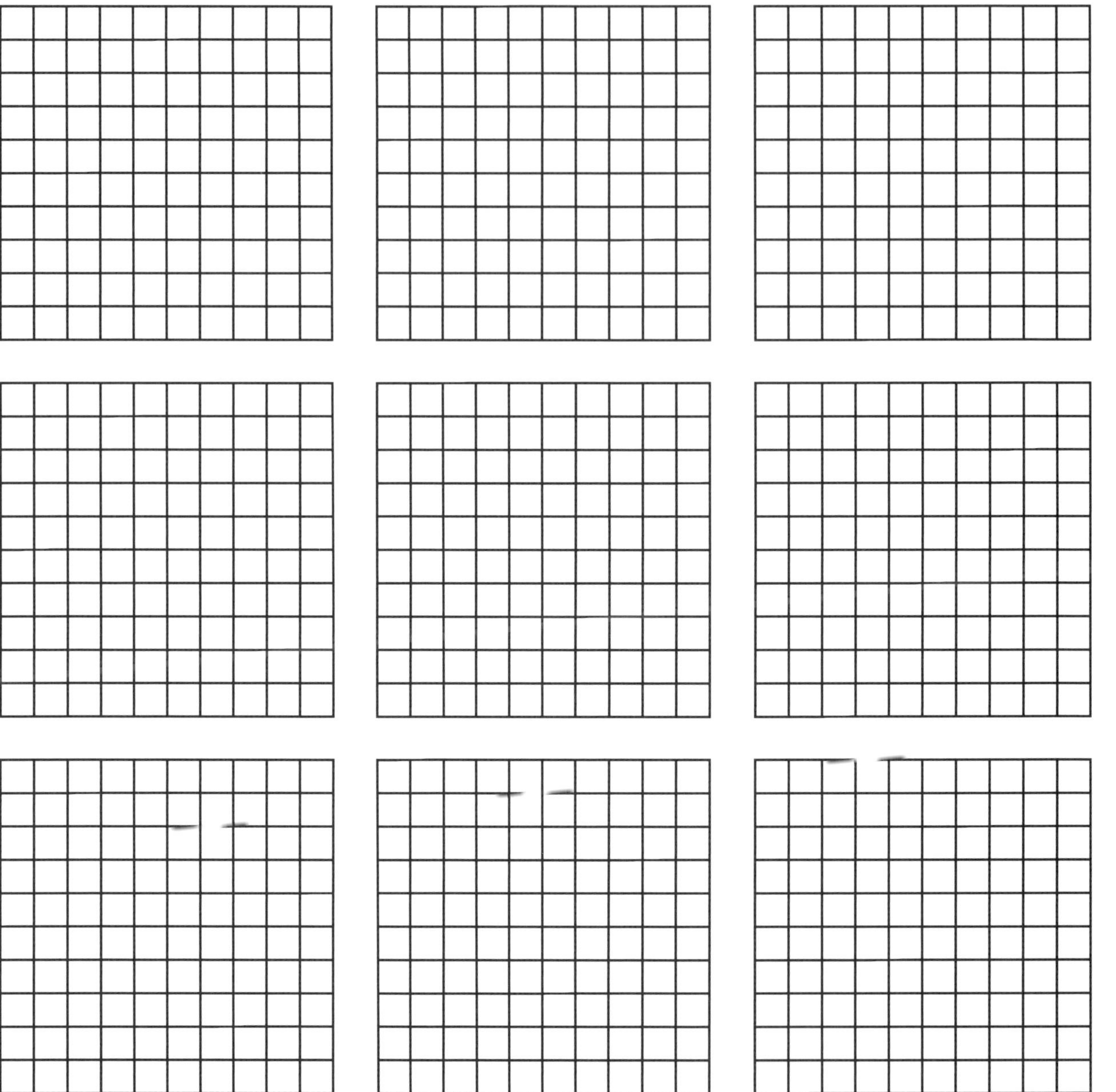

Decimal Representations
Recording Sheet

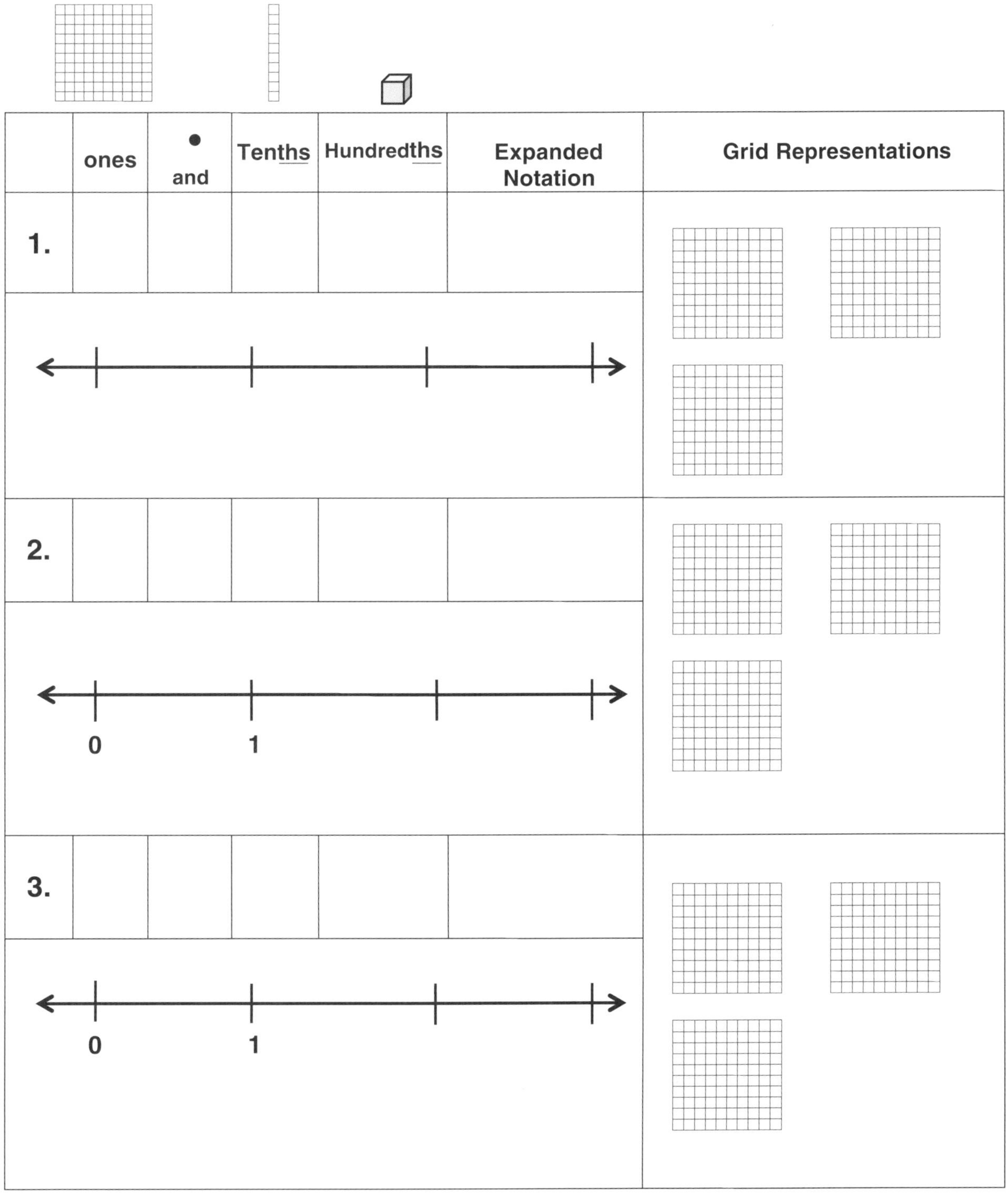

Decimal Representations
Recording Sheet

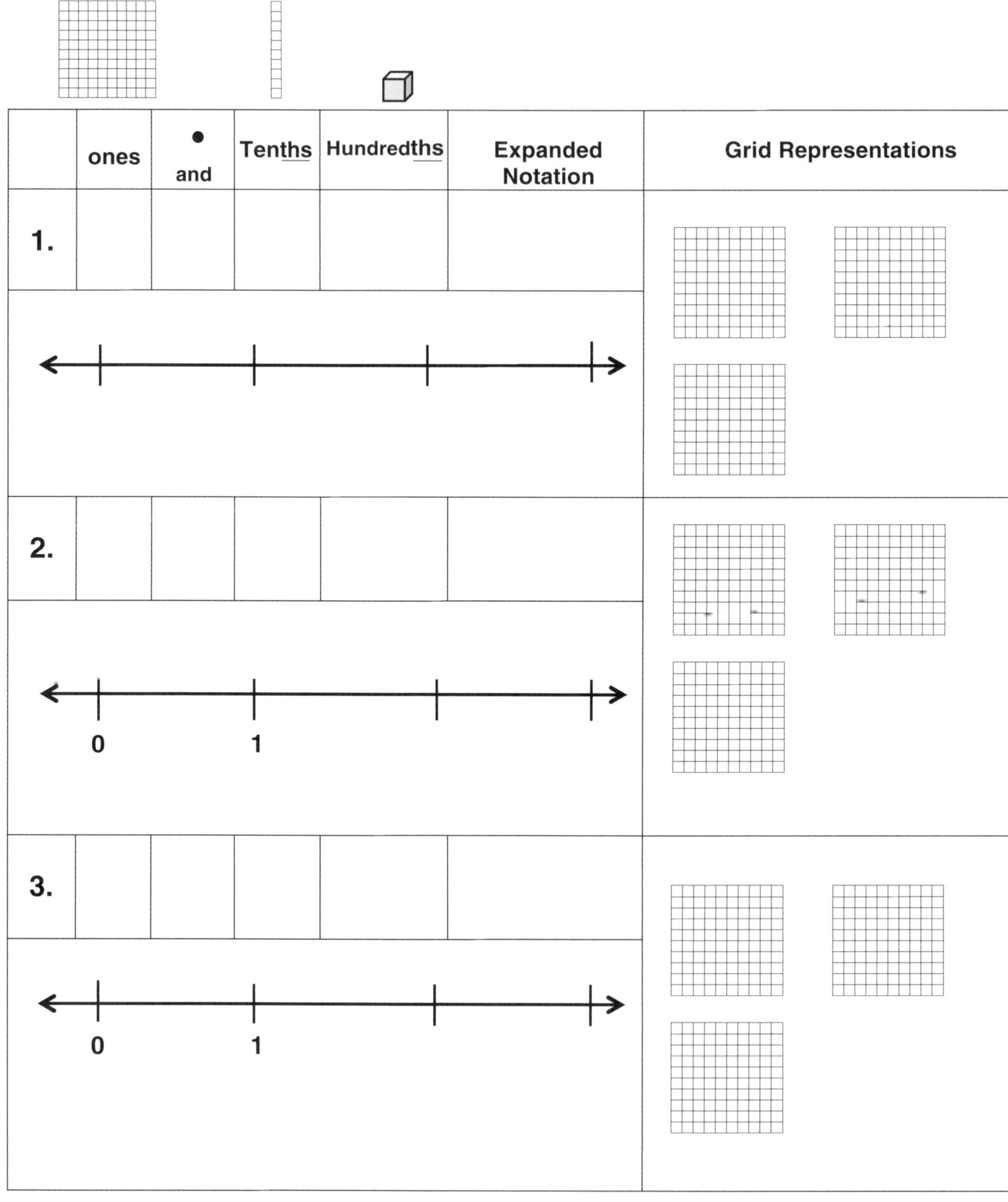

	ones	• and	Tenths	Hundredths	Expanded Notation	Grid Representations
1.						
2.						
3.						

$\frac{1}{2}$-inch Grid Paper

$\frac{1}{2}$-inch Grid Paper

$\frac{1}{2}$-inch Grid Paper

Symbols

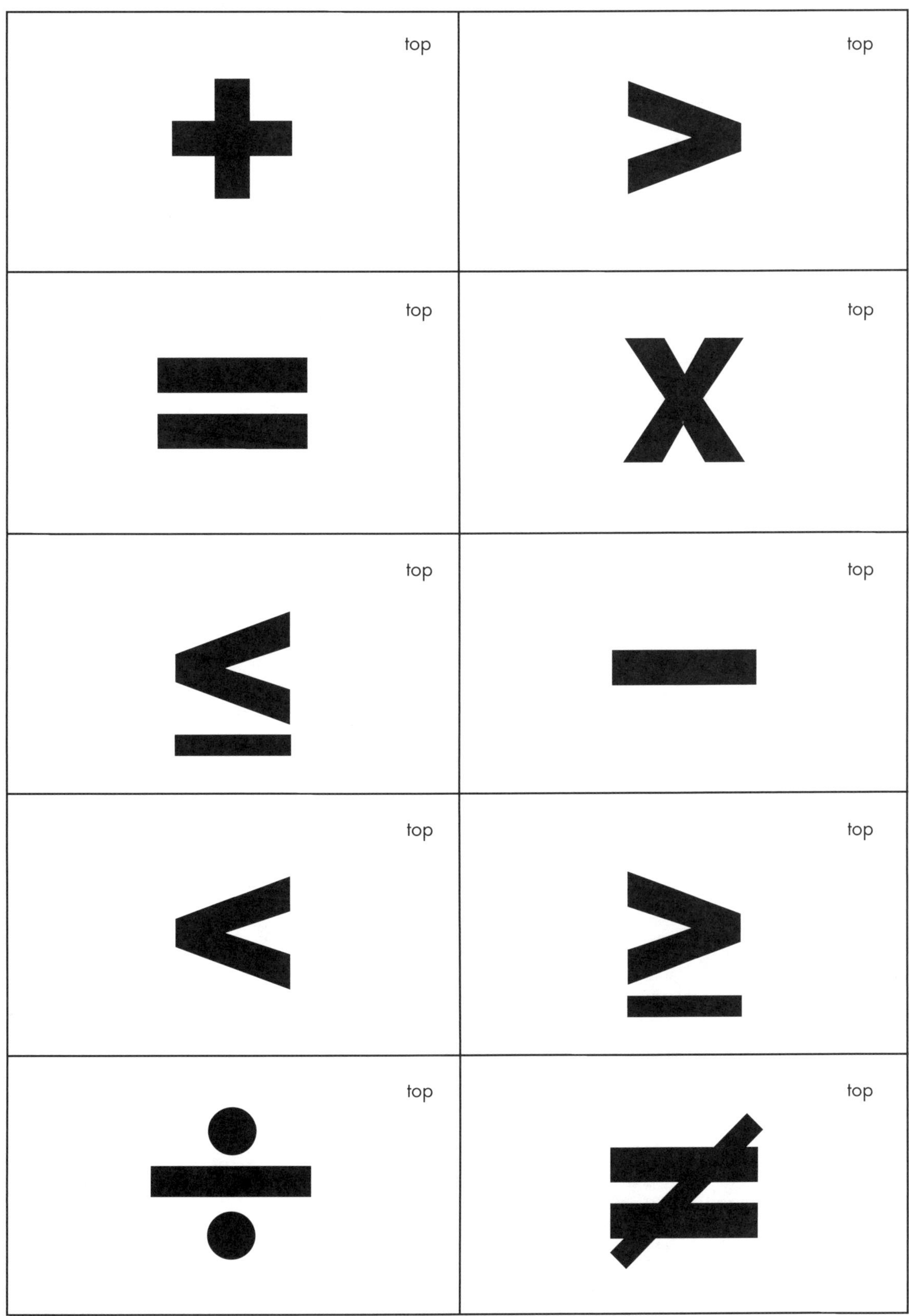

True, False, and Open Sentences

Always True	Sometimes True	Never True

a. $0 \times 2 = \square \times 0$	b. $3 + \square = \square + 3$
c. $15 - 7 = 16 - 8$	d. $2 \times \square = \square + \square + \square$
e. $\square \times 9 = (\square \times 10) - (\square \times 1)$	f. $89 = \square + 80$
g. $\square = 1 \times \square$	h. $16 \div 8 = 8 \div 16$
i. $\square \times 0 = 0$	j. $8 + 2 = 3 + 8$

True, False, and Open Sentences

(continued)

k. 12 = 12	**l.** 24 ÷ 2 = □ + 3
m. 1 ÷ □ x □ = 1	**n.** (5 x 6) x □ = (5 x □) x 6
o. 8 + 5 = □ + 8	**p.** □ x 12 = (□ x 10) + (□ x 2)
q. 15 – 7 = 7 – 15	**r.** □ = □ + 0
s. (5 – 3) – 1 = 5 – (3 – 1)	**t.** 0 = □ – □

Open Sentences

a. $8 + 7 = \square + 6$

b. $8 \times 7 = \square \times 7 + 7$

c. $18 + 22 = 32 + \square$

d. $\square = 12$

e. $8 + 7 = 15 + \square$

f. $10 + 8 + \square = 12 + 9$

g. $\square + 15 + 25 = 17 + 28$

h. $73 + 56 = 71 + 59 - \square$

i. $12 \div 4 = [8 \div \square] + [4 \div \square]$

j. $66 \div \square = (60 \div 6) + 1$

0	1	2	3	4	5	<u>6</u>
7	8	<u>9</u>	10	11	12	13

True or False Number Sentences

a.	b.
$3 \times 7 = 7 + 7 + 7$	$6 \times 4 = 4 + 4 + 4 + 4$
c.	d.
$7 \times 8 = (2 \times 8) + (5 \times 8)$	$8 \times 6 = 8 \times 5 + 6$
e.	f.
$9 \times 7 = 10 \times 7 - 7$	$9 + 6 = 10 + 5$
g.	h.
$37 + 56 = 39 + 54$	$33 - 27 = 34 - 26$
i.	j.
$93 = 9 + 30$	$94 = 80 + 14$

Hundred Chart Puzzle Pieces

1	2	3	4	5	6	7	8	9	10
11	12	13	14	15	16	17	18	19	20
21	22	23	24	25	26	27	28	29	30
31	32	33	34	35	36	37	38	39	40
41	42	43	44	45	46	47	48	49	50
51	52	53	54	55	56	57	58	59	60
61	62	63	64	65	66	67	68	69	70
71	72	73	74	75	76	77	78	79	80
81	82	83	84	85	86	87	88	89	90
91	92	93	94	95	96	97	98	99	100

Race to 100 Tens Strips

10
10
10
10
10
10
10

Race to 100 Fives Strips

5	5
5	5
5	5
5	5
5	5

Race to 100 Action Cards

+10	+10	+10
+10	+10	+20
+20	+20	+30
+30	+5	+5
−10	−10	−10
−20	−5	−5

Race to 100 Question Cards

How many more do you need to reach 100?	How many more do you need to reach 100?	How many more do you need to reach 100?
How far from 50 are you?	How far from 50 are you?	How far from 50 are you?
What is 10 *more* than what you have right now?	What is 10 *more* than what you have right now?	What is 10 *more* than what you have right now?
What is 10 *less* than what you have right now?	What is 10 *less* than what you have right now?	What is 10 *less* than what you have right now?
What is 5 *more* than what you have right now?	What is 5 *more* than what you have right now?	What is 5 *more* than what you have right now?
What is 5 *less* than what you have right now?	What is 5 *less* than what you have right now?	What is 5 *less* than what you have right now?

Sums of More Than Ten Cards

7 + 5 =	5 + 6 =
4 + 8 =	8 + 7 =
9 + 3 =	9 + 7 =
7 + 4 =	6 + 7 =
9 + 6 =	8 + 5 =

Ten-Frame Cards

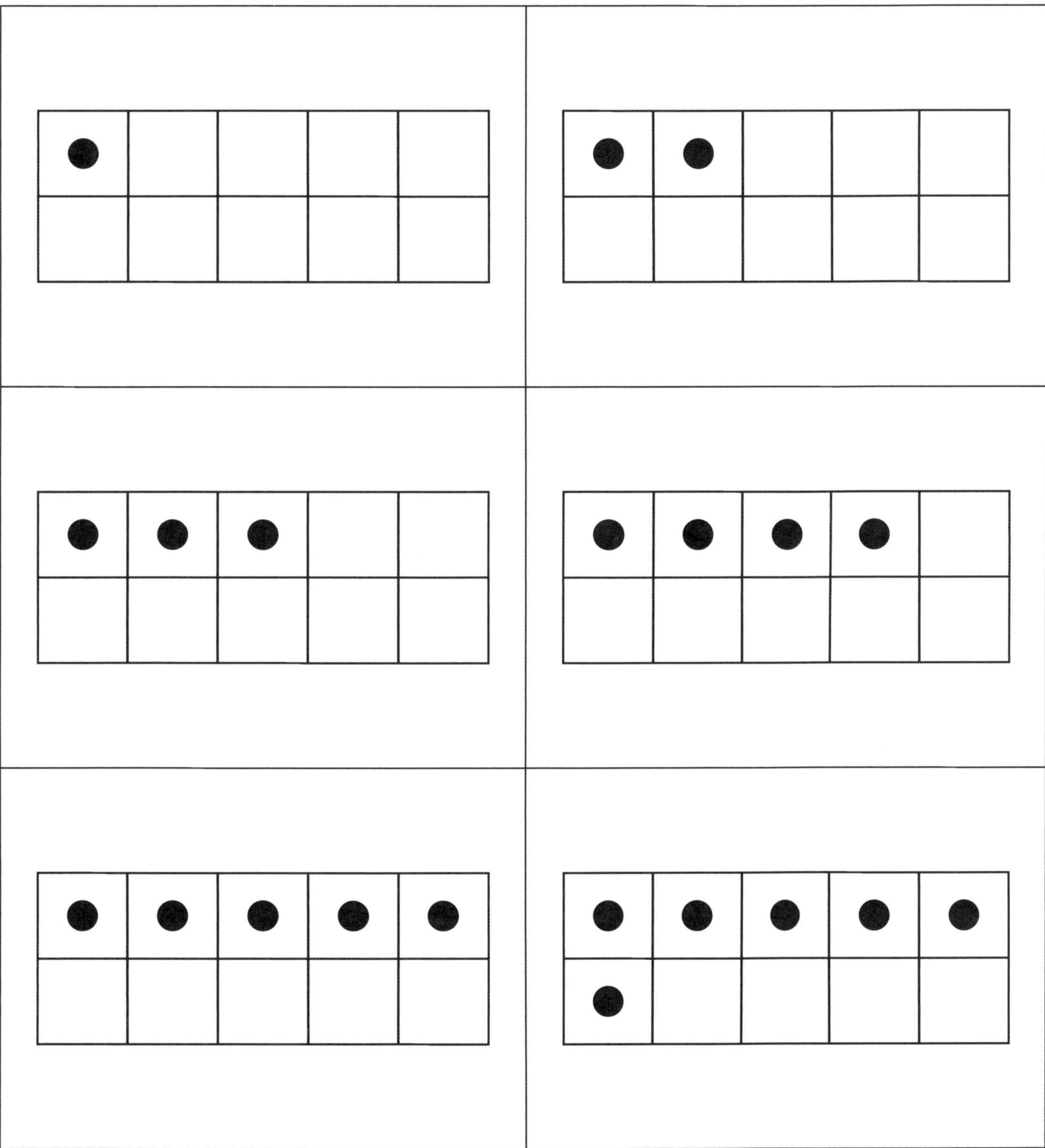

Ten-Frame Cards

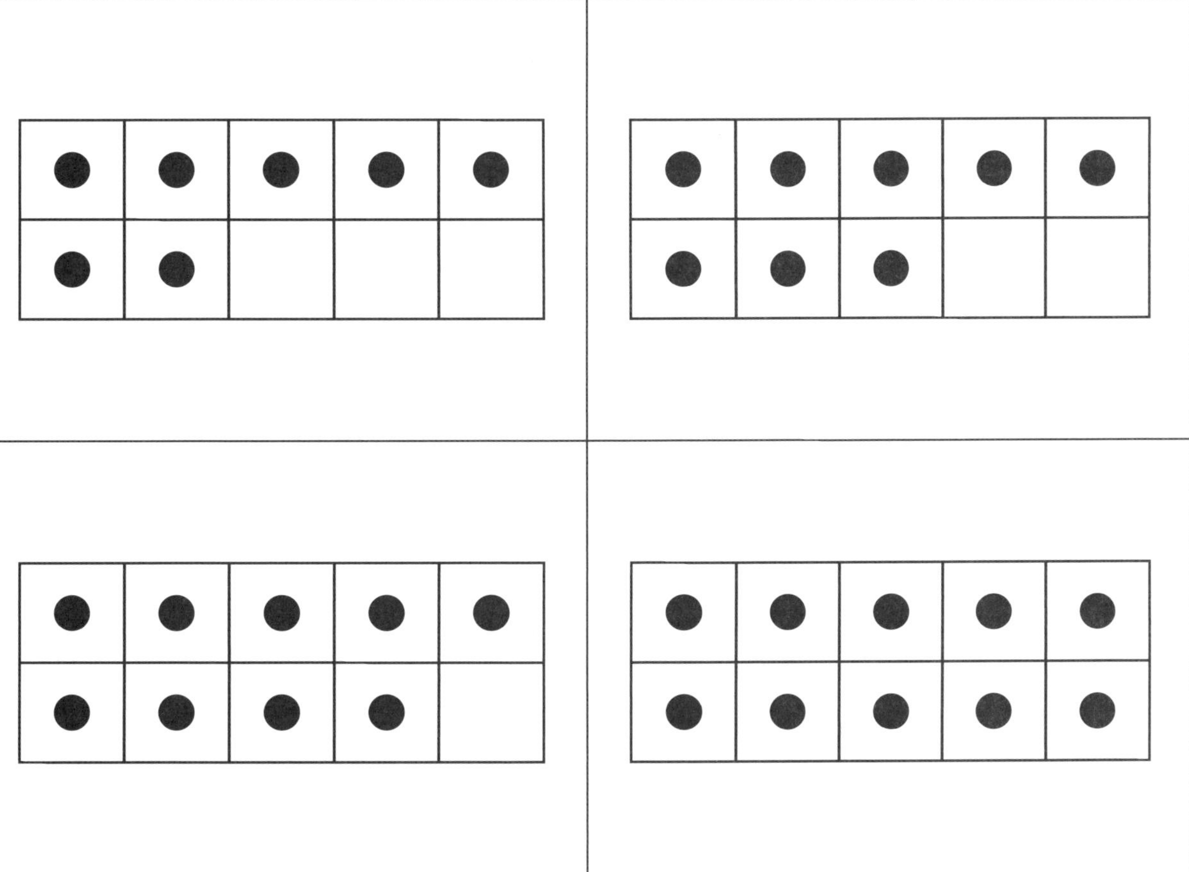